LifeLight

"In Him was life, and the life was the light of men." John 1:4

1 and 2 Samuel

LEADERS GUIDE

CONCORDIA PUBLISHING HOUSE • SAINT LOUIS

To anoint is to apply oil to consecrate a person who has been chosen for the Lord's service. Samuel heard the requests of the Israelites for a king. He obeyed the Lord by anointing first Saul, and then David, Jesse's youngest son, to be king of Israel. We, too, have been anointed, or chosen by divine rite, into the family of God, but our anointing is through Holy Baptism. We are chosen not to be kings or queens, but heirs to the inheritance of eternal life in Christ Jesus, the true Anointed One.

This fresco showing Samuel anointing David (ca. third century AD) was found in the synagogue of the ancient city of Dura-Europos, Syria, in the late 1930s. It is one of more than fifty paintings found there that tell the story of God's people in the Old Testament.

3558 S. Jefferson Ave., St. Louis, MO 63118-3968
1-800-325-3040 • www.cph.org

Written by Steven Teske

Edited by Brian Chisamore

Cover: Samuel anoints David, fresco, ca. 239 AD / © Art Resource, NY

This publication may be available in braille, in large print, or on cassette tape for the visually impaired. Please allow 8 to 12 weeks for delivery. Write to Lutheran Blind Mission, 7550 Watson Rd., St. Louis, MO 63119-4409; call toll-free 1-888-215-2455; or visit the Web site: www.blindmission.org.

Manufactured in the United States of America

1 2 3 4 5 6 7 8 9 10 21 20 19 18 17 16 15 14 13 12

Contents

Introduction

Welcome to LifeLight

A special pleasure is in store for you. You will be instrumental in leading your brothers and sisters in Christ closer to Him who is our life and light (John 1:4). You will have the pleasure of seeing fellow Christians discover new insights and rediscover old ones as they open the Scriptures and dig deep into them, perhaps deeper than they have ever dug before. More than that, you will have the pleasure of sharing in this wonderful study.

LifeLight—An In-depth Study

LifeLight is a series of in-depth Bible studies. The goal of LifeLight is that through a regular program of in-depth personal and group study of Scripture, more and more Christian adults may grow in their personal faith in Jesus Christ, enjoy fellowship with the members of His body, and reach out in love to others in witness and service.

In-depth means that this Bible study includes the following four components: individual daily home study; discussion in a small group; a lecture presentation on the Scripture portion under study; and an enhancement of the week's material (through reading the enrichment magazine).

LifeLight Participants

LifeLight participants are adults who desire a deeper study of the Scriptures than is available in the typical Sunday morning adult Bible class. (Mid-to-older teens might also be LifeLight participants.) While LifeLight does not assume an existing knowledge of the Bible or special experience or skills in Bible study, it does assume a level of commitment that will bring participants to each of the nine weekly assemblies having read the assigned readings and attempted to answer the study questions. Daily reading and study will require from 15 to 30 minutes for the five days preceding the LifeLight assembly. The day following the assembly will be spent reviewing the previous week's study by going over the completed study leaflet and the enrichment magazine.

LifeLight Leadership

While the in-depth process used by LifeLight begins with individual study and cannot achieve its aims without this individual effort, it cannot be completed by individual study alone. Therefore, trained leaders are necessary. You fill one or perhaps more of the important roles described below.

The Director

This person oversees the LifeLight program in a local center (which may be a congregation or a center operated by several neighboring congregations). The director

- serves as the parish LifeLight overall coordinator and leader;
- coordinates the scheduling of the LifeLight program;
- orders materials;
- convenes LifeLight leadership-team meetings;
- develops publicity materials;
- recruits participants;
- maintains records and budgeting;
- assigns, with the leadership team, participants to small discussion groups;
- makes arrangements for facilities;
- communicates outreach opportunities to small-group leaders and to congregational boards;
- follows up on participants who leave the program.

The Assistant Director *(optional)*

This person may assist the director. Duties listed for the director may be assigned to the assistant director as mutually agreeable.

The Lecture Leader

This person prepares and delivers the lecture at the weekly assembly. **(Lesson material for the lecture leader begins on p. 9.)** The lecture leader

- prepares and presents the Bible study lecture to the large group;
- prepares worship activities (devotional thought,

hymn, prayer), using resources in the study leaflet and leaders guide and possibly other, outside sources;

- helps the small-group discussion leaders to grow in understanding the content of the lessons;
- encourages prayer at weekly leadership-team and discussion leaders meetings.

The Small-Group Coordinator *(optional; the director may fill this role)*

This person supervises and coordinates the work of the small-group discussion leaders. The small-group coordinator

- recruits with the leadership team the small-group discussion leaders;
- trains or arranges for training of the discussion leaders;
- assists the director and discussion leaders in follow-up and outreach;
- encourages the discussion leaders to contact absent group members;
- participates in the weekly leadership-team and discussion-leaders equipping meetings;
- provides ongoing training and support as needed.

The Small-Group Discussion Leaders

These people guide and facilitate discussion of LifeLight participants in the small groups. **(Lesson material for the small-group leaders begins on p. 47.)** There should be one discussion leader for every group of no more than twelve participants. The small-group discussion leaders are, perhaps, those individuals who are most important to the success of the program. They should, therefore, be chosen with special care and be equipped with skills needed to guide discussion and to foster a caring fellowship within the group. These discussion leaders

- prepare each week for the small-group discussion by using the study leaflet and small-group leaders guide section for that session **(see p. 47)**;
- read the enrichment magazine as a study supplement;
- guide and facilitate discussion in their small group;
- encourage and assist the discussion group in prayer;
- foster fellowship and mutual care within the discussion group;
- attend weekly discussion leaders training meetings.

Leadership Training

LifeLight leaders will meet weekly to review the previous week's work and plan the coming week. At this session, leaders can address concerns and prepare for the coming session. LifeLight is a 1½-hour program with no possibility for it to be taught in the one hour typically available on Sunday mornings. Some congregations, however, may want to use the Sunday morning Bible study hour for LifeLight preparation and leadership training. In such a meeting, the lecture leader and/or small-group coordinator may lead the discussion leaders through the coming week's lesson, reserving 5 or 10 minutes for problem solving or other group concerns.

While it requires intense effort, LifeLight has proven to bring great benefit to LifeLight participants. The effort put into this program, both by leaders and by participants, will be rewarding and profitable.

The LifeLight Weekly Schedule

Here is how LifeLight will work week by week:

1. Before session 1, each participant will receive the study leaflet for session 1 and the enrichment magazine for the course. The study leaflet contains worship resources (for use both in individual daily study and at the opening of the following week's assembly) and readings and study questions for five days. Challenge questions will lead those participants who have the time and desire a greater challenge into even deeper levels of study.

2. After the five days of individual study at home, participants will gather for a weekly assembly of all LifeLight participants. The assembly will begin with a brief period of worship (5 minutes). Participants will then join their assigned small discussion groups (of twelve or fewer, who will remain the same throughout the course), where they will go over the week's study questions together (55 minutes). Assembling together once again, participants will listen to a lecture presentation on the readings they have studied in the previous week and discussed in their small groups (20 minutes). After the lecture presentation, the director or another leader will distribute the study leaflet for the following week.

Closing announcements and other necessary business may take another five minutes before dismissal.

In some places some small groups will not join the weekly assembly because of scheduling or other reasons. Such groups may meet at another time and place (perhaps in the home of one of the small group's members). Those congregations may record the lecture given by the lecture leader at the weekly assembly and duplicate it for use by other groups meeting later in the week.

3. On the day following the assembly, participants will review the preceding week's work by rereading the study leaflet they completed (and that they perhaps supplemented or corrected during the discussion in their small group) and by reading appropriate articles in the enrichment magazine.

Then the LifeLight weekly study process will begin all over again!

Recommended Study Resources and Worship

The Lutheran Study Bible. St. Louis: Concordia Publishing House, 2009. This resource contains more than 26,000 study and application notes, a most thorough reference guide (pp. lxv–cx), and over 90,000 cross-references, as well as a 31,000-entry concordance, maps, charts, and timelines.

Concordia Self-Study Bible, New International Version. St. Louis: Concordia Publishing House, 1986. Interpretive notes on each page form a running commentary on the text. The book includes cross-references, a 35,000-word concordance, full-color maps, charts, and timelines.

Roehrs, Walter R., and Martin H. Franzmann. *Concordia Self-Study Commentary*. St. Louis: Concordia Publishing House, 1979. This one-volume commentary on the Bible contains 950 pages and is tailored for lay use.

The Concordia Organist is a 31-CD collection of pipe-organ accompaniments for all the hymns and liturgical music in *Lutheran Service Book*. St. Louis: Concordia Publishing House (order no. 99-2264). Use these CDs for worship hymn accompaniment.

Every Voice a Song: Pipe Organ Accompaniment for 180 Hymns and Liturgy. St. Louis: Concordia Publishing House. Use this music CD for worship hymn accompaniment.

The Word of the Lord Was Rare

1 Samuel 1–6

Preparing for the Session

Central Focus

In Samuel's time, and in our time as well, knowledge of God's Word may be lacking even among those who are surrounded by God's gifts of grace.

Objectives

That participants, led by the Holy Spirit working through God's Word, will

1. remember and rejoice in the power of God's Means of Grace—His Word and His Sacraments;
2. realize that faith is not guaranteed by mere exposure to the Means of Grace; and
3. resolve to be active in the use of the Means of Grace through regular Bible reading and active membership in a faithful congregation.

Note for the small-group leaders: Lesson notes and other materials you will need begin on page 49.

For the Lecture Leader

Session Plan

Worship

Begin the session with the hymn printed in the study leaflet. Accompaniments are available in denominational hymnals, such as *Lutheran Service Book* or *Lutheran Worship*. (Note: Concordia Publishing House has available *The Concordia Organist*. All the initial worship hymns in the LifeLight courses are included in this resource. It's especially helpful for mission congregations and small parishes. See the list of study resources on page 7.) Follow with this prayer:

Prayer

Jesus Christ, Head of the Church, You call Your people through Your Word and Your Sacraments and keep us united with You by the same Word and Sacraments. By Your Holy Spirit, keep us faithful to You through these Means of Grace. Guide us that we never take them for granted or ignore them, for apart from You we cannot live, and these are the ways You have chosen to keep us close to You. We ask this in Your holy name, the precious name of Jesus, our Savior. Amen.

Lecture Presentation

1 Introduction

Ray Bradbury was a twentieth-century writer most known for his short stories and novels of science fiction. In some of his writing, such as the novel *Fahrenheit 451*, Bradbury imagined a future society in which knowledge was banned and all books were burned. In other stories, though, Bradbury suggested the opposite approach: he described a society run by people who hid the truth by providing so much information that citizens were unable to sort through it all and discover what is important and what does not matter. So far, at least, it seems as though the twenty-first century resembles this second vision of Bradbury far more closely than his depiction of violent censorship.

People in today's world are all but drowning in information. Every week, the news warns us of new risks and dangers in our lives. We hear and read so many warnings that few of us really know how to measure risk and danger, or how to avoid the real threats while not worrying about the smaller and less likely problems. Science and history and other ways of understanding the world are presented to us with such a bewildering variety of approaches and viewpoints that we often find it hard to know what to believe. As a result of this relentless barrage of information, our opinions are not necessarily determined by truth. Rather, it seems that most people will often make up their minds what to believe first, and then they seek the books and Web sites and television shows that confirm them in their beliefs. News about the present and predictions about the future are offered in exactly the same fashion. No idea is so outlandish and bizarre that it is not somewhere presented as truth, with just as much conviction and aura of authority as any genuine truth.

2 Starving though Surrounded by Abundance

Speaking of the bizarre and outlandish, imagine a society where people were starving to death even though they were surrounded by food. Does that sound ridiculous to you? Perhaps it does. But of course, as ludicrous as it sounds, even this scenario does not require all that much in the way of imagination. All we have to do is to consider our present society. Western civilization has made food—good nutritious food—more available than ever before in the history of the world. Many people eat healthy diets every week, yet the abundance of food has also made the distortion of healthy diets more possible than ever before.

We can think of any number of examples of this. Some people experiment with faddish diets that promise weight loss and other benefits through recommendations of dubious value. Following these diets, a few people actually destroy their health and their bodies, seeking an image presented in society as ideal, but far from what their bodies were meant to be. At the same time, many more people satisfy their cravings for sweets and fats and salt, taking advantage of the highly advertised abundance of such foods. These people forget that our cravings for such foods are appropriate only in a world where food is not abundant and where most food comes from grains and fresh vegetables—the world where most people live today and nearly all people have lived in past centuries. Desires for sweets and salt led people to correct and balance their diets because such things were rare. Today, in our part of the world, those foods are easily acquired. The unfortunate result is that some people tend to over-eat these unneeded foods and avoid the food that is good for them. We can very easily find ourselves starving, in a sense, while being surrounded by food. Food, just like information, surrounds us and confuses us so badly that we cannot sort the good from the bad or learn to be good stewards of the bounty that is ours.

We see a similar problem at work in the Book of 1 Samuel. At the time Samuel was born, we are told in the Bible, "the word of the LORD was rare" (1 Samuel 3:1). This is a very significant statement that needs to be understood properly. First of all, we can note that reading this one statement may cause us to overlook the abundance of blessings God was giving to His people at that time. Those blessings He had given them were truly amazing! Only a few generations after the time of Moses, families could easily pass down to their children the memory of the escape from Egypt, the giving of the Law at Mount Sinai, and the entry into the Promised Land. The written books of Moses and of Joshua belonged to the Israelites. They had a record of all that God had said and done in the lives of their ancestors, Abraham, Isaac, and Jacob. They had a complete record of the life of Moses and of God's commands, given at Mount Sinai. The history of the way God kept His promises and gave the land of Canaan to the tribes of Israel was inscribed and preserved for God's people. God had commanded that the members of the tribe of Levi be scattered throughout the land, living in every town and village to teach the people God's Word and to remind them of what God had said and done.

More than that, God's people had visible reminders of the Lord and His promises. They had the tabernacle, built in the days of Moses according to God's commands, which had accompanied God's people into Canaan and now stood at Shiloh. Within that tabernacle was the ark of the covenant, a symbol of the throne of God among His people. In that ark were the Ten Commandments, inscribed on tablets of stone, along with other reminders of the history of Israel. At that tabernacle, regular sacrifices were offered to the Lord, which were pictures of the coming Savior and His sacrifice that would save the world. The ark and the tabernacle, the priests and the sacrifices, all were there to be God's message to His people—a reminder of judgment but also a promise of salvation.

Therefore, when we read that God's Word was rare, we can recognize what that really means. His Word was rare not because people needed special revelations from the Lord, but because they were ignoring the message God already had given to them.

3 Abusing What Was Holy (1 Samuel 1–3)

God's Word was rare not because it was absent, but because it was simply ignored. As bad as that was, there was also something even worse. God's Word was not merely being ignored; it was being abused. The sons of the high priest were guilty of the most flagrant abuse of God's Word. They used the sacrifices of God's people as opportunities to take what they wanted from the people (see 1 Samuel 2:12–17, 22). They ignored their father's warning that such abuse of the people whom God loved, and of God Himself, would bring judgment upon them.

There were also other, less visible ways, that the Word of God was being ignored and abused. Samuel, the boy whose life was dedicated to serving the Lord, did not even recognize the name of the Lord. When God called to him repeatedly, Samuel thought each time that Eli the priest was calling him and ran to ask Eli what he wanted. Eli eventually realized that God was calling the boy and told him what to say: (1 Samuel 3:9) "Speak, LORD, for Your servant hears." (Notice that there the word *LORD* is printed in our Bibles all in capital letters. When we see this, we know that the word actually found in the original Hebrew is not the title "Lord," but rather the very name of God, usually rendered as either Jehovah or Yahweh. Our English Bibles generally follow an ancient tradition of, as an act of reverence, substituting another word for that holy name. The title is then usually printed in all capital letters so that the reader knows that this substitution has been made. That is what we see here in 1 Samuel 3.) Eli used that special name of God, the name God explained to Moses in Exodus 3:14, the name that means "I AM WHO I AM." Samuel did not know this name, so when God called to him again, he actually forgot God's name and said only, (1 Samuel 3:10) "Speak, for Your servant hears." For this reason, the Book of 1 Samuel says that (3:7) "Samuel did not yet know the LORD, and the word of the LORD had not been revealed to him." Surrounded by the tabernacle, the ark of the covenant, the priests, and the sacrifices, Samuel still was a stranger to God. In the midst of pure spiritual food, he was starving.

God had answered the prayer of Hannah and provided her with a son, as she had asked. God poured out His grace on Samuel by calling out to him, even three times. He made him a messenger of the Lord, speaking God's Word to sinners, warning them of the cost of their sins, but also providing opportunity for repentance and forgiveness.

4 Judgment and Grace (1 Samuel 4–6)

God's grace is always more powerful than His judgment. God's judgment is real, because He must condemn sin and punish sinners. Sin damages and destroys the good things God has made. Sin is bad for the people God loves. Sin, as rebellion against God, takes the side of death against life and takes the side of hate against love. God must speak against sin. When sinners refuse to repent, God must bring the punishment He has threatened. Yet God is patient, not wanting to judge and condemn and destroy, but wanting to rescue and restore. Therefore, at the center of His plan is a Savior. God poured out His wrath against sin upon His Son. God allowed Jesus of Nazareth to go to the cross, to suffer and to die so that all the punishment that sinners deserve could be consumed in the obedience of Christ. Thanks be to God, God's judgment and God's grace meet at the cross. Grace triumphs, so that even the worst of sinners can be rescued, forgiven, and brought back into God's family.

God's grace is met at the cross. For that reason, every reminder of God in the Bible (both Old and New Testaments) is a reminder of the cross. The animals that were sacrificed to God were pictures of the death of Jesus. Even the tabernacle and the ark of the covenant were reminders of Jesus, the Son of God, dwelling among God's people and bringing God's mercy into their lives. Of course, the sacrifices, the priests, the tabernacle, and the ark were more than pictures or reminders of God; they had the real power of God's presence and of His grace and mercy. Therefore, every rejection of these gifts and every distortion of these gifts was a genuine attack upon God and upon the Gospel of Jesus Christ. God's judgment on the sons of Eli was potent, not because their sins were worse than all other possible sins, but because their sins blocked the very stream of forgiveness that God had established for His people.

The ark of the covenant was a source of mercy for those who approached it in faith; but, for those who did not have faith in God, it was a source of judgment and destruction. When the Philistine army captured God's ark, they brought a destructive power into their cities. Their own god toppled and broke to pieces before the presence of the God of Israel. Judgment hit their cities as a plague because they were lacking faith in God. When God's ark was returned to Israel, it brought comfort and blessing. For those who knew God's promises and had faith in Him, the presence of ark was good and not destructive.

5 Pharisees and Philistines

Similar to Old Testament times, Christendom today is filled with powerful promises of God's presence. Cities in Europe and the Americas are dominated by beautiful church buildings. Bibles are available in nearly every bookstore. Radio, television, and the Internet all share messages about Christ. Yet in the midst of this spiritual plenty, millions are starving to death spiritually. Like Samuel, they do not know the Lord, even though His presence fills everything that surrounds them.

Among the many places identified as churches and labeled with the name of Jesus Christ, nearly every heresy rejected by the Bible and by the Early Christian Church can be found. The attitude of the Pharisees is common, focusing upon obedience to God's commands, even at the price of resisting or rejecting the guarantee of forgiveness through the promised Savior. Holy things are despised and removed, or they are allowed to remain and are ignored. Some groups bearing Christ's name have taken away the Word of God, declaring it to be nothing more than human opinions, antique and curious but not meaningful or powerful. Some groups bearing Christ's name have taken away the sacraments of the Church, changing them into acts of obedience that demonstrate our love for God rather than acts of grace that deliver God's love and forgiveness to us. Some groups bearing Christ's name have changed the church into a social club, or into a political-interest group, or into a lodge that encourages good deeds while accepting anyone, regardless of their beliefs about God and Christ. Even today, while surrounded by so many reminders, the Word of the Lord can still be rare.

The Word of God is powerful, because God is present in His Word. Yet God speaks two messages in His Word, messages that together tell a complete story, even though at times they appear to contradict each other. The Law of God reveals the reason people were made, what we were put on earth to do. That same Law shows us that we have fallen short of God's plans and deserve His punishment. We have not met the expectations of our Maker. The Gospel tells us that God loves us in spite of our flaws. He wants to rescue us and so has sent His Son to be our Savior. Through the work of Jesus, we are restored to God's original plan. The Law requires obedience, but the Gospel tells us that Jesus has fulfilled the commands for us. The Law threatens punishment, but the Gospel tells us that Jesus has taken away our guilt and has been punished in our place. In the end, we are transformed by the Gospel so we can perform the deeds of the Law; anyone who tries to please God by obeying the Law without relying on the power of the Gospel will still fall short of God's plan and will be condemned by the Law.

Those who seek power from God's Word without faith in Christ are like Philistines capturing the ark of the covenant without faith in the God of Israel. God's power will only humble and destroy those who approach Him by means of the Law. Their false confidence in their own good works will be shown to be empty as those good works crumble in the face of God's demand for perfection. The Law threatens sinners with death; only the Gospel of the cross of Jesus Christ brings life. Even Holy Baptism and Holy Communion have no power to save unbelievers by themselves. Both sacraments become effective through the Word of God, which gives participants the benefits of forgiveness, life, and salvation. When unbelievers reject these gifts from God and fail to recognize Christ or to remember His work as Savior, even these Sacraments can, like the ark of the covenant, convey judgment and death rather than grace and life.

Conclusion

God's people deserve wrath and judgment for the many ways we have abused and distorted His Word and His other gifts to us. In spite of our sins, God remains patient. He continues to call to the people He loves, as once He called to Samuel. The Word of God has not lost its power, even where it is distorted or ignored. The water of Holy Baptism still washes away sins, and the bread and wine of Holy Communion still convey Christ's body and blood, bringing forgiveness and life to those who eat and drink with faith in Christ's promises. Jesus is still found wherever two or three gather in His name, and He remains with His people always, even to the ends of the earth. We can know that where His Word is preached correctly and His sacraments are observed in purity, Christ is present. Where sinners fall short of perfection and purity, Christ is willing to forgive and to claim His people in spite of their sins. Though He threatens judgment against all who despise and reject His grace, He also promises grace and mercy to all who turn to Him in faith. Even that faith is His gift, given by the power of His Word. Those who trust in the Lord remain secure in all His promises, even to all eternity.

Concluding Activities

Speak a closing prayer, make any necessary announcements, and distribute study leaflet 2.

Appoint for Us a King

1 Samuel 7–12

Preparing for the Session

Central Focus

Our attitude toward the authority of human government reflects and reveals our attitude toward the Lord of lords.

Objectives

That participants, led by the Holy Spirit working through God's Word, will

1. understand the reasons why Samuel did not want to anoint a king over Israel;
2. understand the reasons why God chose to place a king over Israel; and
3. see the relationship in their lives between human authority and God's authority.

Note for the small-group leaders: Lesson notes and other materials you will need begin on page 51.

For the Lecture Leader

Session Plan

Worship

Begin the session with the hymn printed in the study leaflet. Accompaniments are available in denominational hymnals, such as *Lutheran Service Book* or *Lutheran Worship*. (Note: Concordia Publishing House has available *The Concordia Organist*. All the initial worship hymns in the LifeLight courses are included in this resource. It's especially helpful for mission congregations and small parishes. See the list of study resources on page 7.) Follow with this prayer:

Prayer

Heavenly Father, You sent Your Son, Jesus Christ, to be King of kings and Lord of lords. Grant that we may faithfully follow His rule. As we look forward to the eternal kingdom of Your new creation, help us also to respect those who rule over us in this world, honoring them for the sake of Your Son, our King, Jesus Christ. In His name we pray. Amen.

Lecture Presentation

1 Introduction (1 Samuel 7–8)

Disagreements within governments and about governments are part of life in the contemporary world. In the United States, two large political parties dominate most elections, while small parties strive also for their voices to be heard. In other countries, governments are formed in Parliament by a coalition of parties when one party cannot win the majority of seats in an election. People expect a voice in their government; they vote, they write letters to their leaders, they publish messages in newspapers or on the Internet, and they gather in rallies to call attention to their political opinions. Some people speak to support those in positions of power, while others speak to replace those in positions of power with new leaders. Only rarely, though, does anyone advocate a completely different style of government. Very rarely in the history of the world have the citizens of a country had an opportunity to determine the form of government under which they would live.

During the lifetime of Samuel, the Israelites seized just such an opportunity. The people were ready for a change; they thought that their lives would be greatly improved under a different form of governance. The people met with Samuel and asked him to choose a king to rule over them. They wanted a king! This is amazing when we recall all that the Israelites had gone through over the centuries. Their ancestors had been slaves in Egypt, living under the authority of the Pharaoh, but God had set them free from slavery—from slavery under a king. At Mount Sinai, God claimed the Israelites as His people and promised to be their God, but He spoke to them through Moses and defended the authority of Moses to lead the people. When Moses died, Joshua was chosen to replace him. After Joshua died, the Lord raised up other judges to lead Israel. Now, Samuel was the last of the judges. The Israelites wanted a different form of government. They wanted to have a king.

2 Reasons for and against Having a King (1 Samuel 8:10–18)

When Samuel heard what the people asked, he argued against them. Samuel did not want Israel to fall under the rule of a human king; he wanted them to continue to regard the Lord as their only king. Even after God had forced Samuel's hand and told Samuel to do as the people wished, Samuel still argued with them and told them that having a king was a bad idea, that they would not be better off. However, in the end, the people got precisely what they wanted, and they even got it with God's permission. Samuel, though, very quickly came to regret the fact that the people got what they wanted. He must have been tempted more than once to say to them, "I told you so."

The people wanted a king for three reasons: First, they feared the disorder in Israel due to the lack of a central government. For generations, God would raise up judges where and when He chose, and the people often had to wait years for help against their enemies. Sometimes, the Israelites did not even recognize the judges that God had chosen and so they ignored them or resisted their leadership. Tribes of Israel at times even fought against one another, sometimes because of confusion due to the fact that they had no central authority other than God Himself. Second, Israel was prey to bad rulers because they lacked a king. This had been the case repeatedly. For instance, the son of Gideon, and the sons of Eli the high priest, and even the sons of Samuel sinned against God and against the people. When things like this happened, the people saw no authority to help them resist such evil. Third, the people of Israel wanted to be like the other nations around them. All those nations were succeeding, in the eyes of Israel, under the leadership of kings. Since the office of king seemed to work well for the neighbors, Israel also wanted to be ruled by a king—surely, they assumed, then their lives would be better.

To counter these arguments, Samuel issued several warnings about what harm a king might do to the lives of the people. First, Samuel warned, their sons and daughters would be drafted into service to the government. And not just their sons and daughters, but even their animals would be forced into government service and taken away from them. A king would reorganize the nation for the benefit of the government, and the personal rights of the people would suffer. They would lose control over their families and the things that were theirs, all for the benefit of the strong central ruler whom they requested.

A second warning of Samuel was that the king would require taxes of the people. Samuel threatened that the king would demand 10 percent of their income and the best of their property. A 10-percent tax might not seem very high by modern standards, but Samuel chose that figure to remind the people that the king would make claims equal to those made by God Himself.

Samuel's third warning was that the Israelites would become slaves to their king. A 10-percent tax and the loss of the best of the harvest, the best animals, the best servants, and even their sons and daughters, were all seen by Samuel as mere symptoms of the real problem. The real problem was that by choosing to be ruled by a king, the Israelites were surrendering their freedom. With God as their only king, they were free; but, with a human king placed over them, Samuel was convinced, the people of Israel would no longer be free.

3 Rules for a King (1 Samuel 8:19–22; Deuteronomy 17:14–20)

Samuel objected to the request of the people, but God told him to give the people what they asked for. Samuel's words about the dangers of a king were so harsh that the Israelites actually apologized for their request and asked to be forgiven, but God had approved of what they asked. While Moses was still alive, God had anticipated this request. In the farewell sermon of Moses, we find that God had prepared His people for the day when they would have a king. In Deuteronomy 17:14–20, God listed four requirements that the Israelites should keep in mind when they chose a king for themselves.

First, their king would actually be chosen by God—and only by God. The people were not free to choose a king for themselves. When they wanted a king, they had to accept the man God had chosen for them. They were not to accept a volunteer who offered to be their king. If they were to be ruled by a king, then they had to be ruled by a man that God had chosen to be king.

Second, their king would be a fellow Israelite. God did not permit His people to seek a king from outside the nation God had chosen to be His own people. It might have seemed reasonable to select a king from the royal family of some neighboring nation, to select a man who had been trained in the ways of royalty, but God did not permit this choice. He insisted that any king to rule over His people had to be a descendant of Abraham, Isaac, and Jacob, the patriarchs of Israel.

Third, the king was not to do all those things that Samuel said a king would do. He was forbidden by God to amass many horses, many wives, or much wealth. Especially, he was forbidden to turn to Egypt to acquire such things, since God had set His people free from slavery to the Egyptian rulers. The king was not to be a burden to His people, but instead was expected to be a servant to His people. Therefore, expecting the nation to support many horses, many wives, or a luxurious palace was contrary to the spirit that God required of a king.

Fourth, the king was to be guided by the Word of the Lord. Especially, he was to be guided by the Book of Deuteronomy. He was to keep that message from God close at hand, to study it often, and to be prepared to apply it to all the challenges that faced him as he ruled God's people. The words God spoke to His nation through Moses were the words that would tell a king how to rule and would guide him in all his responsibilities as he took care of the chosen people of God.

4 Three Kings

Saul was the first king to rule the twelve tribes of Israel. Saul was chosen by God. God communicated His choice in several ways so that Samuel and the people of Israel, as well as Saul himself, would have no doubt about God's choice. Saul was an Israelite, of the tribe of Benjamin. He began his career humbly, without demanding wealth from the people he ruled. He appears to have been a genuine servant to Israel and to have been guided by the Word of God, at least early in his rule.

Before he died, though, Saul had become a failure as a king. As we read the rest of the Book of 1 Samuel, we will see Saul fall short of God's plan in two important ways. Saul will begin to defy the Word of the Lord, deciding which of his enemies to destroy and which to spare, rather than obeying the commands that God gave to Saul. Also, Saul will begin to perform tasks that are not his job to do. Saul will do the work of a priest, offering animals to God before battle. That is not a trivial matter. By combining the tasks of king and priest, Saul will make of himself more than God intended for him to be. Only one person in Israel would combine the offices of priest and king, and that chosen ruler was not Saul.

Therefore, we will read about a second king over Israel in the Books of 1 and 2 Samuel. David also was chosen by God to rule the Israelites. David also was one of God's people, from the tribe of Judah. David also was a humble king, although he did have several wives and did build a palace. Still, David did not go to the extent that foreign kings did in gathering wealth of various kinds at the expense of his people. David was guided by God's Word, though at times he strayed from that Word and disobeyed God's commands. David, in the end, can be seen to resemble the king of Deuteronomy's commands more closely than he did the king of Samuel's warnings.

In the Book of 1 Kings, we also learn about Solomon, the son of David, the last king to rule all of the twelve tribes of Israel. He was chosen by God and was an Israelite, but Solomon proved to be essentially the kind of king that Samuel threatened would take power over the people of God. He did acquire many horses, many wives, and much wealth. He did gather the wealth of the nation to himself, although much of his wealth came from foreign nations rather than from taxes on Israel. He wandered away from the commands of God, building temples to the false gods of his wives and even worshiping those gods in those temples. Solomon's sins were so serious that, after his death, God allowed civil war in Israel, splitting the tribes into two countries that spent centuries competing with each other and sometimes fighting against each other.

5 Another King

Samuel was right to warn the Israelites about the problems they would face under the rule of a king. After all, we can recall that God did intend for the Israelites to have a king. These earlier kings, like Saul and David, in spite of their sins and their failures, were preparing God's people to be ruled by a greater king. Such a king finally would come, a thousand years after Saul and David. He would be chosen by God and anointed by Him. He would be an Israelite, from the tribe of Judah and the family of David. He would not acquire the wealth of the world, would not gather horses or wives or money, and would not force people to serve Him. Instead, He would be a servant to the people. He would be guided by God's Word and would never stray from God's commands. He would even be what Saul tried to become—a king who would also serve as a priest for the people of Israel.

All these promises were fulfilled in Jesus, the Son of God and the Son of David. Though He is as human as were His forerunners, Jesus never sinned or fell short of God's plan. The commands of God vividly describe the life that Jesus lived. When tempted by Satan in the wilderness, Jesus did not fall into temptation. Instead, three times He quoted the words of Deuteronomy to the tempter, proving Himself to be the king described in that book, the king who was to be guided by the words of that book. Pontius Pilate and his soldiers would mock Jesus, calling Him King of the Jews, but Jesus truly is the King of the Jews. More than that, He is King of kings and Lord of lords, in charge of all people, and the source of authority in every nation under the sky. He is even our King who also serves as our great High Priest. For it was Christ Himself who performed for us the greatest priestly service that there ever could be. It was given to the priests to offer sacrifices to atone for the sins of the people and to intercede with God on their behalf. Our God fulfilled these duties to the utmost in our Lord Christ. It is He who offered Himself as the eternal, once-for-all sacrifice for the sins of the entire world. And it is Jesus who prayed to the Father on our behalf on the night in which He was betrayed, and still continues to intercede for us always.

We cannot consider these three Old Testament kings without recalling that God has placed them before us to draw our attention to the greater—even infinitely greater—King whom He promised would come to us. Therefore, we can easily see that Saul, anointed by Samuel to be the first king of Israel, was a picture of Jesus, that ultimate king of Israel. Keeping this in mind will help us understand one of the repeating themes in the later part of the Book of 1 Samuel. What can jump right off the page at us—and be a little difficult for us to appreciate—is David's tremendous respect for Saul, even when Saul does not deserve that respect. David will not harm or defy the one who was anointed of God for two reasons. First, in a very practical vein, David sets an example of how he wants to be regarded when he is king. Second, in a more significant sense, David respects the authority of Saul, not only as king over Israel, but also as one anointed to represent the Christ, the future King of the Jews.

We should bear in mind that this is true not just of Saul and David, but of all kings. All kings, even bad kings, rule with authority that comes ultimately from God. All leaders, even bad leaders, rule with authority that comes ultimately from God. Even when their authority comes from a ballot box, from the consent of the people, still the fact that they have authority makes them pictures of Jesus. In a democracy, citizens are able to advise their rulers and even, on occasion, to fire and replace their rulers. According to God's Word, though, Christians are not free to despise their rulers. The respect we show to those in authority reflects the authority we have for Jesus. When we defy, mock, or ignore our rulers, we defy, mock, and ignore our Lord.

This does not mean that we must take the bad with the good. When we are forced to make a choice, "we must obey God rather than men" (Acts 5:29). In our form of government, we often do not need to make such a choice. We can speak against wrong laws without breaking the law. We can respect our rulers even when we disagree with them and choose to vote against them. We can honor Jesus by taking a stand for what is right, while we can also honor Jesus by honoring the authorities who rule over us. Like David, we can refuse to harm the Lord's anointed, while we put all our trust and faith in the Christ, the ultimate Anointed One of the Lord.

Conclusion

Samuel feared that the Israelites were rejecting God by asking for a king. In a sense, they were; but in another sense, they were not. Certainly, by rejecting the organization of governance that God had already established for them, they were despising one of His bountiful gifts and asking for something that would be harmful for them, as Samuel warned them. Yet, as we have seen, there was another side to this. Without even realizing it, by asking for a king, the people were pointing forward to our Lord Jesus, the King of kings, who would come among them. They were inviting God to continue His rule over His people, just in a different way. Though they said that they wanted to be like the people around them, adopting the same form of government that the other nations had, still there would remain a significant difference between them and the other nations. Though now they were ruled by a king, God's people continued to be different because the King of all creation was promised and guaranteed to rise up from among them.

Concluding Activities

Speak a closing prayer, make any necessary announcements, and distribute study leaflet 3.

In the Name of the Lord of Hosts

1 Samuel 13–18

Preparing for the Session

Central Focus

David prevailed over Goliath, not because he believed in himself or in his cause, but because he trusted God's promises.

Objectives

That participants, led by the Holy Spirit working through God's Word, will

1. comprehend the politics and military strategy involving the Israelites and Philistines three thousand years ago;
2. recognize David's faith in God's promises as his source of strength, confidence, and victory; and
3. apply the same confidence in the Lord to their personal battles with evil, sin, and temptation, recognizing Christ's victory in all these struggles.

Note for the small-group leaders: Lesson notes and other materials you will need begin on page 53.

For the Lecture Leader

Session Plan

Worship

Begin the session with the hymn printed in the study leaflet. Accompaniments are available in denominational hymnals, such as *Lutheran Service Book* or *Lutheran Worship*. (Note: Concordia Publishing House has available *The Concordia Organist*. All the initial worship hymns in the LifeLight courses are included in this resource. It's especially helpful for mission congregations and small parishes. See the list of study resources on page 7.) Follow with this prayer:

Prayer

Lord Jesus Christ, three thousand years ago, You blessed David and granted him victory over Goliath. Two thousand years ago, You won the final victory over sin and evil and death. Grant us a share in that victory today, confident that Your promises are as true for us today as they were for Your people in ancient times. Amen.

Lecture Presentation

1 Introduction

It is a scene we have all seen at one time or another. It has occurred with such regularity that it is something of a cliché. Before the game was even half over, the announcers were already comparing the teams to David and Goliath. The larger school had a much better-funded athletic program, more big-name players on scholarship, and a much better reputation for sports success, and yet they were losing to the smaller school. The score grew closer in the second half, but the larger school never managed to tie the score. When the game ended, the fans from the smaller school went wild in victory celebrations. Meanwhile, the announcers analyzed the game thoroughly from start to finish, repeatedly asking the reason for the surprising outcome. Had the larger school been overconfident, failing to take the smaller school seriously, looking ahead too soon to their next game? Was the larger school overrated, not as good as everyone thought, showing weaknesses that other opponents now could exploit? Did the smaller school excel because of excellent coaching or a talented group of players? Did the smaller school get lucky, or did their athletes just want this victory more than the athletes from the larger school? Regardless of the reason behind it, the seemingly impossible had happened. The underdog had been victorious; and it was amazing to watch.

This kind of scenario happens often, and few people can resist comparing such a contest to the battle of David and Goliath. Although those two warriors faced each other on a battlefield roughly three thousand years ago, their names continue to be remembered whenever a seemingly small or weak force defeats—or nearly defeats—a larger or better-equipped force. The comparison is, of course, not limited to athletic victories. Many of us may remember that the survival of George Bailey's Building and Loan in the face of Mr. Potter's assault is compared to a David-and-Goliath fight in the movie *It's a Wonderful Life.* Other times, in fiction or in real life, when a single individual or a small group of people has succeeded in a fight against a large, impersonal corporation, comparisons are made to the fight of David against Goliath. Even in politics, candidates who are unknown, inexperienced, and poorly funded are often compared to David and their better-known, more-experienced, and better-funded opponents are compared to Goliath. It is a very common comparison.

2 The War between God and Evil (1 Samuel 17)

It is probably safe to say that, of all the names in the Bible, few are better known in Western civilization than those of David and Goliath. Most people know the essential story, and most people think they know what it means. Two moral lessons are frequently drawn from the account of David's fight against Goliath. The first moral lesson most people see in the story is that it is important for the individual to stand for what is right and to resist what is wrong, no matter how much stronger the wrong side appears to be. The second moral lesson many people derive from this event is that anything is possible for the person who truly believes in himself or herself.

The writers of the Bible might agree that God's people should defend what is right and resist what is wrong, even when the wrong side seems stronger than the right side; though they might also hesitate to agree wholeheartedly with that. However, the writers of the Bible would definitely disagree that anything is possible for the person who truly believes in himself or herself. The problem with both of these statements is that they overlook two of the key verses in 1 Samuel 17 that describe the confrontation between David and Goliath. When he first hears Goliath threaten the armies of Israel, David asks, (v. 26) "Who is this . . . that he should defy the armies of the living God?" Later, David says to Goliath, (v. 45) "I come to you in the name of the LORD of hosts, the God of the armies of Israel, whom you have defied." This clearly shows us that David does not win because he believes in himself; David wins because he believes in God. Furthermore, we see here that the battle is not so much a matter of right against wrong as it is part of the war of God against evil.

The account of David and Goliath is also remembered and repeated by people who understood its place in the description of the war between God and evil. Today, many people tend to generalize such conflicts as "the battle between good and evil," but that is not really what we are referring to. That description suggests an idea that good and evil are opposing forces, equal for the most part, fighting for control of this world. Several important truths can easily fade away and be forgotten when that description is used. When they think of a battle between good and evil, people can easily forget that God is almighty and that all the forces of evil have no chance at all of ever defeating Him. When they think of a battle between good and evil, people forget that God is perfectly good, and that everything that falls short of perfection is on the side of evil. When they think of a battle between good and evil, people regard themselves as basically good, assuming that their small mistakes and shortcomings do not really matter.

In the real war, the battle between God and evil, God is almighty, and evil cannot defeat Him. God is perfect, but the people He loves are sinners who often fight against Him. God battles evil not just to win a victory, but to rescue sinners and to restore them to perfection. He also plans to rescue the world from sin and restore it to perfection. The battle between God and evil is decided not in a massive military confrontation in the valley of Armageddon. Rather, it took place on a cross placed by Roman soldiers on a skull-shaped hill near the gate of Jerusalem. And there that conflict was decided absolutely, for all time and even for all eternity.

3 Ancient Warfare (1 Samuel 17:1–3)

Of course, the war between Israelites and Philistines was waged one thousand years before that cross was planted. And if we just quickly read through this account, it seems to be only loosely connected to the war between God and evil. However, in spite of that, it is worth our effort to consider it more thoroughly.

In some ways, it is a little difficult to tell the two sides apart. In the war between Israelites and Philistines, both sides consisted of sinners who were enemies of God apart from the saving work that Jesus would accomplish on the cross. Both nations came to the land of Canaan from elsewhere. The Israelites came first from the city of Ur in Mesopotamia (modern Iraq) and more recently as slaves escaped from Egypt. The Philistines, on the other hand, came from the islands of the Mediterranean Sea. The Philistines were a loose confederation of five cities built near the coast, while the Israelites consisted of twelve tribes only recently united under a king. The Philistines held their power partly by maintaining a monopoly on iron tools and weapons, but even with that advantage, they had not succeeded completely in controlling the Israelites.

What did this conflict look like? It can be hard for us to picture. Warfare has changed so much in the last centuries that the battles of three thousand years ago are difficult for us to imagine today. Although some movies depict ancient warfare in a fairly accurate manner, many more movies create unrealistic images of ancient warfare for dramatic purposes. A common form of battle in ancient times involved two armies, each equipped with armor and weapons, running toward each other at full speed. The winners would crush the losers, and the losers would suffer many more casualties than the winners. Several factors could make a difference in this kind of battle. Better armor and better weapons obviously could make one side stronger than the other. Better training and stronger individual soldiers would also make a difference. An army that was well-trained and worked together as a group could usually defeat a band of individuals who had not learned how to fight as a team. There were many other factors involved in these combats; for instance, even the landscape could make a difference. An army running downhill had two distinct advantages: their momentum gave them more speed and power than their opponents running uphill, and they would also be able to strike in a downward direction rather than upward at their enemy.

For this reason, two armies could reach a stalemate by camping on nearby hills of about the same height. Neither army would want to start the attack against the other, because the army that began running first would reach the valley first and be heading uphill when the lines met. Initiating the battle would put an army at a disadvantage, so they might find it more prudent to stay in place and try to taunt the other side into attacking. The Israelites and Philistines seem to have achieved exactly that kind of stalemate when David came to visit his brothers at the battlefield. Both sides seemed to view the tactical situation the same way. For forty days (v. 16), the two armies camped on their hills; neither wanted to leave the battlefield and concede the fight, and neither wanted to begin the attack and fight at a disadvantage.

4 Chosen People (1 Samuel 17:4–47)

Yet, for all the similarities between the two groups, there was one tremendous difference. The biggest difference between the two groups had nothing to do with how they were armed, or how they fought, or where their people originally came from. Instead, the biggest difference between the two groups clearly was the fact that the Israelites were chosen by God. We can recall from the Book of Genesis that God had told Abraham to move from Ur to Canaan. Later, God had brought the descendants of Abraham up from Egypt. At Mount Sinai, He had promised them, (Leviticus 26:12) "I will . . . be your God, and you shall be My people." In the wilderness, He had fed them manna, bread from heaven, and provided them water from a rock. When they first entered the land of Canaan, He had worked miracles to give them victory over the Canaanite tribes. He had promised to continue granting them victory over all their enemies as long as they remained faithful to Him, but the Israelites broke their side of that contract with God. They worshiped the false gods of the Canaanites. As a result, God allowed them to lose to their enemies, intending to remind them of their sins and of His promises so they would return to Him and be faithful.

David remembered the promises of God. He knew that, when God's people were faithful to Him, He would not break His promises to them. When David heard the boasts of Goliath and knew that Goliath was relying on the Philistine gods, David was confident of his victory. He expected to win and was not afraid of losing, not because he believed in himself and not because he knew that he was right, but because he trusted the promises that God had already spoken to His chosen people, the Israelites.

Goliath, on the other hand, trusted in the gods of the Philistines, but he also believed in himself. From all appearances, Goliath was a true believer in himself. He knew that he was bigger and stronger than any other fighter on the battlefield. He also knew that he was a trained warrior who had a natural advantage in any hand-to-hand combat. Most likely, Goliath had never lost a fight during his military career. He had every reason to believe that the Philistines were meant to be rulers of Canaan and that the Israelites were meant to be their servants. If the moral of the account of David and Goliath was about believing in yourself and fighting for what you think is right, Goliath should have been the winner of this fight.

After all, who is David? He has been introduced three times in the Book of 1 Samuel. He is the youngest son of Jesse, chosen by God and anointed by Samuel as a future king of the twelve tribes of Israel. He is a musician who is brought to Saul from time to time to comfort the king with music. He is a shepherd boy whose older brothers are fighting in the army but who has not yet been called into military service. Each of these facts is a different facet in the career of David. Like Moses before him, David is being prepared by God for a unique combination of tasks that will require many skills and many experiences for him to succeed.

Who is David? We find that the single theme uniting the different pictures of David—musician and shepherd and future king—is the fact that he trusts God's promises. We see that so clearly in this account of his combat with Goliath. When he fights Goliath, he does not need the king's armor and sword. They would only get in his way. He does not enter battle unarmed, though; David brings his sling and five stones. David understands that faith in God and His promises does not mean sitting down and doing nothing. He could have sat and waited for the Lord to overcome Goliath and the Philistines with a miracle. Instead, David, because he trusted God, volunteered to do what he could to serve God and to help God's people. He prepared himself, not in the ways that other people thought would be best, but in the way that he knew would work best for him. All the while, he was relying on the sure and certain promises of God.

5 Not a Cucumber (1 Samuel 17:48–58)

Was David frightened, facing Goliath on the battlefield? Most likely so. Did he know without any doubt that he was going to win and Goliath was going to lose? David speaks with confidence, but he must have known that sometimes God allows His people to suffer and to face defeat. As we have all observed, bad things do happen to good people in this sinful world, and sometimes the bad guys win. Yet, in spite of that, David was willing to rely on the promises of God and to do his best. His knowledge that he had been anointed king and had been told by Samuel that he would rule Israel must have given David extra confidence as he carried his sling and his five stones toward Goliath.

Of course, if David had simply been fighting a metaphor, he would have been more confident. If Goliath had been only a symbol of big, powerful companies, David would not have been frightened. Goliath was not a symbol or a metaphor, any more than he was a cucumber: Goliath was a large, powerful, trained warrior who had every intention of carrying through on his threat to kill David and overpower the Israelite army.

On his own, David would not have defeated Goliath; frankly, David wouldn't have had a chance. He had less training and less equipment, and he did not even believe in himself. But David was not left to his own devices; he was not alone. No, David was not alone; he was fighting for Israel, the chosen people of God; therefore, God was indeed with him. Meanwhile, Goliath clearly had taken sides against Israel. Goliath trusted in false gods. By mocking God's people, Goliath was mocking God Himself. For this reason, God granted David success. Because of the promises He already had made to the people of Israel and to David, God granted David success. The musician and shepherd and future king come together in a red-headed boy carrying a sling into battle on a hillside in ancient Israel.

Conclusion

In the dark days of the American Civil War, President Abraham Lincoln was asked whether God was on his side or the side of the Confederate States. Lincoln replied that the important question was not whether God was on his side, but whether he was on God's side. For Goliath, Lincoln's observation certainly is true. Goliath failed because he deliberately took the side opposed to God and to God's people. For David, the lesson is not quite so simple, but is far more significant. David was without question on God's side. But far more important than that was that God had already promised to be on David's side; and so David was sure to be victorious.

Far more beneficial than any moral about believing in oneself, this is what we may draw from the account of this battle; and it is something in which we may always find comfort and certainty. God had promised to be on David's side, bring him victory, and raise him up as king over God's people. Though it may seem like an insignificant piece of ancient history, this has tremendous importance for us. For as we see recounted for us in the New Testament, and as was prophesied all throughout the Old Testament, a thousand years after Goliath fell, God took David's side again. For then, Jesus Christ—the Son of God and also the Son of David—faced an even greater enemy. Jesus did not fight a giant, but He did fight sin and evil and death. Jesus won that fight, and won eternally the war between God and evil. Because He is on our side today, we know that we share in the victory He won that day. We are winners forever, because God is on our side.

Concluding Activities

Speak a closing prayer, make any necessary announcements, and distribute study leaflet 4.

David and His Merry Band of Outlaws

1 Samuel 19–24

Preparing for the Session

Central Focus

David, as an outsider, can be regarded as a picture of Christ and of His grace, prevailing over evil and also over the Law of God and its condemnation of sinners.

Objectives

That participants, led by the Holy Spirit working through God's Word, will

1. comprehend the relationship of Saul and David and observe its complexity;
2. see Jesus as the Savior who frees sinners from the condemnation of the Law; and
3. join with Jesus, not as rebels against God's Law, but as redeemed sinners, set free by the work of the Savior.

Note for the small-group leaders: Lesson notes and other materials you will need begin on page 56.

For the Lecture Leader

Session Plan

Worship

Begin the session with the hymn printed in the study leaflet. Accompaniments are available in denominational hymnals, such as *Lutheran Service Book* or *Lutheran Worship*. (Note: Concordia Publishing House has available *The Concordia Organist*. All the initial worship hymns in the LifeLight courses are included in this resource. It's especially helpful for mission congregations and small parishes. See the list of study resources on page 7.) Follow with this prayer:

Prayer

Lord Jesus Christ, You entered this sinful world to defeat sin and evil and to set us free from the chains of sin and the condemnation of Your Law. Gather us to You, redeemed and forgiven, that we may share in Your victory and rejoice to be Your people. Amen.

Lecture Presentation

1 Introduction

Most people in the English-speaking world are familiar with the story of Robin Hood. Most would regard him as a basically good man. He broke an unfair rule and was forced to hide in Sherwood Forest to protect himself from the law. There, he gathered a band of outlaws like himself, who not only survived but prospered in the forest. Stealing from the rich and giving to the poor, Robin Hood and his fellow outlaws earned the gratitude and loyalty of the common citizens, while upsetting the powerful rulers of the land. Yet Robin and the others became so skilled in the ways of the forest and in weaponry (the use of the bow and arrow, the quarterstaff, and similar tools) that they could flaunt their freedom, mocking the authorities and then returning safely to their hiding place in the wilderness.

If there ever was a Robin Hood in medieval England, he was probably far different from the Robin Hood of legend and of recent books and movies. Yet, his story does appear to be based in historic fact. Indeed, the story of Robin Hood resembles that of David, the son of Jesse, who needed to hide in the wilderness to be safe from King Saul and from other powerful enemies. Whether deliberate or not, it appears that some storytellers who repeated and embellished their accounts of Robin Hood borrowed freely from the biblical record. The careers of the two men are different in many ways, of course, yet the story of Robin Hood bears a striking resemblance to the story of David, the son of Jesse and the ancestor of Jesus Christ.

2 Comparing David to Robin Hood (1 Samuel 19–24)

This may not be a comparison that ever occurred to you before. In fact, it may even seem a bit frivolous. Nonetheless, it is worth our consideration. What parallels can we draw between the two men?

David and Robin Hood both are noble warriors forced to hide in the wilderness. Their nobility does not come from being born into a rich and important family; their nobility is more an inner virtue, along with a reputation for doing the right thing. Yet both men have run afoul of the authorities. Both are in danger of being arrested and punished unfairly. Both are forced to hide, and both do manage to hide successfully from those who intend to harm them.

Both David and Robin Hood attract to themselves a band of talented fighters, men who also seem to be opposed to the authority in charge of the land, men who seek an opportunity to strike back and to even the scales of injustice. Some of the mighty men of Israel who fought with David and helped him to rule Israel had already joined him while Saul was still alive. Robin Hood had Little John, but David had Abishai the son of Zeruiah. Robin Hood had Friar Tuck, but David had Abiathar the son of Ahimelech, the priest of Israel. If the mighty men of David did not rob the rich and give to the poor, still they were a blessing to their neighbors, guarding their flocks and herds in the fields and keeping their property safe from attack. David and his men even kept the southern border of Judah safe, attacking the enemies of Israel. Their stronghold on the border between the land of Judah and the land of the Philistines was an ideal place for them to hide in plain sight, able to escape any opposition while still resisting their enemies.

Robin Hood successfully resisted the power of the sheriff of Nottingham, who becomes a comic villain in some versions of the legend. Even King John is sometimes drawn into the story, but the king of England is no better than the sheriff in capturing these outlaws. David also escapes from a king. Saul pursues David in the wilderness, but is never able to capture him. On one occasion, David's men and Saul's army are on opposite sides of the same hill: David knows that Saul is there and uses the hill to escape, but Saul does not realize how near David is. On two other occasions, the groups are so close that David is able to touch Saul. Their story also has potential for comedy, although the stakes are so high—the life of David is in danger—that the humor of the situation is obscured for the reader by the danger David must face.

The seriousness and the danger of the situation definitely strike us as we read of the struggle between David and Saul. The stakes in this conflict are so high. Saul is not the sheriff of Nottingham. He is the king of Israel, chosen by God and anointed by Samuel. However, he has sinned, disappointing God and losing his place in God's plan for Israel. Saul has decided for himself which prisoners will survive and which will be killed instead of obeying God's commands about the nations that fought against Israel. Worse, Saul has added to his duties as king the work of a priest. This offense is worse because only the coming Messiah will hold the jobs of both priest and king. God has rejected Saul as king and has chosen David to replace Saul, but Saul is still alive and still rules over the twelve tribes of Israel.

Saul is a dangerous enemy for David to face. He continues to have the loyalty of most of the warriors of Israel. As head of the government, he makes the laws, and he can declare David to be an outlaw. When he takes the army south to hunt for David, he has the means to destroy David and his band. Saul must be taken seriously in the drama of David's life, because Saul is more dangerous to David at this time than even the Philistines.

Moreover, David has great respect for Saul, the king of Israel. Twice, when he has the chance to kill Saul, he refuses. He regrets even cutting off a corner of Saul's robe, saying, (1 Samuel 24:6) "The Lord forbid that I should do this thing to my lord, the Lord's anointed, to put out my hand against him, seeing he is the Lord's anointed." David actually apologizes to Saul during this circumstance, which also might have been humorous had the stakes not been so high. Saul also apologizes to David and admits that he has been wrong to bring the army of Israel against David, even though this is not the last time that Saul will do such a thing. Saul has committed the greater wrong by pursuing David, but David is the first to apologize to Saul.

David respects Saul because he is the Lord's anointed, the chosen king of Israel. David, who has already been anointed to replace Saul on the throne of Israel, has great respect for the office of king. David respects the office of the king of Israel, not merely because he one day will be king, but because every king of Israel is a picture of the ultimate King, the promised Messiah. This also, of course, is an important difference between David of Bethlehem and Robin Hood: Robin Hood will never become king of England, but David is chosen and anointed to be, one day, king of Israel. And as king of Israel, David will serve as a picture of the Coming One, even the Son of God Himself.

3 David: a Picture of Jesus

This certainly is not a foreign concept to us. We are familiar with David as a picture of Jesus Christ. The writers of the New Testament stressed the identity of Jesus as the Son of David to emphasize this Old Testament image. History was shaped by God to cause Jesus to be born in Bethlehem, the city of David, so He could inherit the throne of His ancestor. Throughout the Gospels, we see men in need calling to Jesus as the Son of David. We also read that He was welcomed into Jerusalem at the beginning of Holy Week with songs celebrating Him as the Son of David and king of Israel. The reign of King David was, without question, pointing the people to the coming eternal Son of David.

Many other kings were reminders of the ultimate King of the Jews; even bad kings can be regarded as distorted pictures of Jesus. But even though there were many kings listed in the Old Testament, David stands out from all the rest. David is special as an image of Jesus because of the other connections between the two men. David was a shepherd who became king and who wrote the famous Psalm that begins "The Lord is my shepherd." Jesus declared Himself to be the Good Shepherd who cares for His sheep. David fought against the champion Goliath and won. Jesus fought against our powerful enemies Satan and evil and death, and He also won.

David may remind us of Jesus in his roles as king, shepherd, and heroic fighter, but can David be like Jesus in his role as outlaw? At first blush, that may seem like an odd thought. Nevertheless, a connection can be established between Jesus and the outlaw David apart from David's future role as king of Israel—so much so that even Jesus Himself mentions the connection and allows us to see Him as the Robin Hood of the New Testament, standing against injustice and defending the poor and needy of the land.

Of course, Jesus, like David, is a mighty hero who eventually will rescue the nation. David will become king of Israel after Saul's death and will defeat the Philistines and other enemies, bringing peace to Israel. Jesus will defeat Satan and sin and death by dying Himself; but after His own death, He will rule the Church—the new Israel—and will bring peace to all His people, peace that surpasses our understanding. As David draws men to him who are anticipating his future rule, so Christ draws believers to Him, even in this sinful world, who are looking forward to eternal life in the promised new creation.

4 Looking Deeper

Looking deeper, though, we find in Jesus Christ a man who is subject to the Law and who yet goes beyond the Law and lives outside of the Law. As the one true Son of God, Jesus knows His Father's will and does His Father's will. As both true God and true man, He accepts and agrees with the commands of His Father. Jesus was born into this world and lived in this world as a substitute for all sinners. He obeyed the Law of God so He could credit every sinner with His obedience. He fulfilled the Law in a way that sinners never can. By fulfilling the Law, Jesus not only obeyed it thoroughly, but He also completed the purpose of the Law. Because He has fulfilled the Law, His people are no longer subject to the Law in the same way that they were before He came.

Certain aspects of the Law (such as rules about food and the Sabbath day) no longer apply to the people of God because of the way that Jesus fulfilled the Law. Consider, for example, Colossians 2:16–17. After discussing our redemption through Christ Jesus, St. Paul then directs our attention to one of the results of that redeeming work of Jesus: "Therefore let no one pass judgment on you in questions of food and drink, or with regard to a festival or a new moon or a Sabbath. These are a shadow of the things to come, but the substance belongs to Christ." These were "shadows" of the coming Christ. In other words, these aspects of the Law are no longer binding upon us. They have passed away because their whole purpose was to be a foreshadowing or a precursor—an Old Testament reality whose principal purpose was to point the people to rely on the promised Christ and the blessings provided through Him. But now that Christ has come and fulfilled the Law, these precursors have found their fulfillment and so have passed away.

Because Jesus has fulfilled the Law, both in His perfect obedience before His death and also by the sacrifice in which He died to pay for all sins, His people now are free from the Law. This does not mean that Jesus sets Christians free to do whatever they want. It means that He sets them free to do whatever He wants. By His death on the cross, Christians have died to sin and are no longer condemned to live in sin. Christians are forgiven all their sins, and that same forgiveness works to transform them into the image of Christ. This transformation has not yet been completed: Christians still sin every day and need God's forgiveness every day. In Christ, and through the promises of Holy Baptism, Christians are forgiven every day and are set free from sin every day. Being set free from sin, Christians also are set free from the Law. No longer is God's Law a burden to control sinners. God's Law brings Christians to repentance, as it also describes for Christians how we are being transformed so we can be more like Jesus.

By fulfilling the Law, Jesus goes beyond the Law. Pure Law would demand that each person receive what he or she deserves, but Jesus takes the suffering we deserve for our sins and grants us the blessings that He alone deserves. Pure Law would deny us a place among God's people now and a place in His new and perfect world, but Jesus grants us both a place among His people today and a place with Him forever. Under pure Law, only Jesus would rise from the grave and go to heaven; all other sinners would go to eternal punishment. Jesus promises a place in heaven to all who trust in Him, and He assures us that His suffering and death on the cross are sufficient to grant eternal life to all the sinners of the world.

5 Jesus as Thief and Outlaw

Is it going too far to call Jesus an outlaw and to compare Him to David the outlaw? It might be going too far if Jesus had never said such things, but Jesus does say such things. More than once, He compares Himself to a thief (Matthew 24:43; Matthew 12:29). Furthermore, Jesus explicitly compares Himself to David the outlaw. When the Pharisees protested the fact that the disciples of Jesus were picking and eating grain on the Sabbath, which was contrary to their interpretation of God's commandment about the Sabbath, Jesus responded, (Matthew 12:3–4) "Have you not read what David did when he was hungry, and those who were with him: how he entered the house of God and ate the bread of the Presence, which it was not lawful for him to eat nor for those who were with him, but only for the priests?" For years, this question bothered me, because it seems as if Jesus is saying that some of God's laws are negotiable, as if morality itself is relative and not absolute. Of course, nothing could be farther from the truth. What Jesus was doing in this incident was not arguing against morality or denying the truth of God's Law but demonstrating His own mission to set people free from the Law and to grant them the freedom of the Gospel.

This point is difficult to see at first, because we crave solid ground on which to stand. We want firm truths on which we can base our lives. We think we have found these in the Law of God, which describes His perfect will and His plan for the world when He created it, which is His plan for our lives. The fact that we have broken the Law, though, means that it no longer can be solid ground for our feet. The solid ground is now the good news of the Gospel, the news of forgiveness and life in Jesus Christ. We are sinners, condemned by the Law, but He is beyond the Law, able to take away our guilt and the punishment we deserve. He replaces our guilt and our punishment with His grace and His blessings.

Would it then be a stretch for us to think of ourselves as "outlaws"? We usually think of an outlaw as someone who is a criminal—a persistent lawbreaker. However, the old use of the word is a little different. An outlaw was someone who, usually as a punishment, had been placed outside the law, in the sense of being outside the law's protection. In a way, we are outlaws as well, but a little differently. It's not that we have been placed outside God's protection, but rather, as a result of Jesus taking our guilt and punishment upon Himself, we are placed outside of the Law's eternal condemnations.

Conclusion

Christ was very much an outlaw, not unlike David. He was an outlaw who was being pursued. If the Law pursues Christ, as Saul pursued David, then we are safer hiding with Christ than we are serving under the Law. Both David and Saul were anointed by Samuel, but David prevailed where Saul failed. Likewise, Christ has redeemed and saved us by the Gospel, whereas the Law, due to our sinfulness, could never bring us to salvation.

So now, rather than serving under the Law, we serve under Christ—outlaws, perhaps, but not lawbreakers. We are still in the wilderness, for Christ has not yet returned in glory to make the world perfect and claim His kingdom in its fullness. The kingdom and the victory and the glory belong to Him already, though, and already He shares with us the blessings He has promised. As we await the fullness of His kingdom, we rejoice in what is to come as well as in what we already have today.

Concluding Activities

Speak a closing prayer, make any necessary announcements, and distribute study leaflet 5.

Four Remarkable Women
1 Samuel

Preparing for the Session

Central Focus

God works through various kinds of people to accomplish His plan in the world.

Objectives

That participants, led by the Holy Spirit working through God's Word, will

1. acknowledge that women, as well as men, have a place in God's plan;
2. understand that the key difference between people is the presence or absence of faith in Christ and His promises; and
3. rejoice to know that even sinners can accomplish important roles in God's plan.

Note for the small-group leaders: Lesson notes and other materials you will need begin on page 59.

For the Lecture Leader

Session Plan

Worship

Begin the session with the hymn printed in the study leaflet. Accompaniments are available in denominational hymnals, such as *Lutheran Service Book* or *Lutheran Worship*. (Note: Concordia Publishing House has available *The Concordia Organist*. All the initial worship hymns in the LifeLight courses are included in this resource. It's especially helpful for mission congregations and small parishes. See the list of study resources on page 7.) Follow with this prayer:

Prayer

God of the universe, You created all things and made them good, but sinful men and women have brought evil and death into the good world You made. You sent Your Son to redeem all people, and You send Your Spirit to bring faith to all people. Grant that all who trust in You and are saved by the work of Your Son see themselves as members of Your holy family, held together by Your grace and not divided by the barriers that separate people in this sinful world, through Jesus Christ, Your Son. Amen.

Lecture Presentation

1 Introduction

The Book of 1 Samuel is, to a very great extent, a heroic book; so much so, in fact, that the heroic men of 1 Samuel are very easy for us to spot. Men such as Samuel, Saul, and David leap off the pages and grab our attention as we read. Others play a supporting role, such as Jonathan, who was Saul's son and David's best friend. In a tale of prophets and priests, kings and warriors, set roughly three thousand years in the past, we might expect men to hold all the starring roles. This makes it all the more noteworthy once we realize that was not the case. We can easily notice, as we read through the book, that 1 Samuel contains some very remarkable women as well.

God's Word has always been about God and all of His people; people from every language and tribe and culture. In other words, God's Word is for everyone—for men and for women, for adults and for children, for the wealthy and for the poor, for the powerful and for the weak. God's Word is meant for all kinds of people, so it should not surprise us that it describes all kinds of people. From that, we can clearly see that, no matter who we may be, we may always learn about ourselves when we study the Scriptures. We learn about ourselves and about the commands of God and the grace of God when we study the lives described in the Bible, even if the language and the culture of those lives was very different from ours today.

2 Hannah (1 Samuel 1:1–2:11)

The Book of 1 Samuel begins with a woman, with Hannah the wife of Elkanah. Clearly, we can see that several aspects of her life are less than ideal. Hannah is, first of all, married to a man who has another wife. Of course, this situation is not unusual in the Bible: Jacob was married to Leah and Rachel, who were sisters, and both David and Solomon had many wives. However, God's intent for marriage seems clear in Eden when He makes for Adam one wife. In both Old and New Testaments, though, God speaks clearly against adultery and other sins of its kind without saying specifically that it is sinful for a man to have two or more wives.

Much time is wasted puzzling over matters that God has chosen not to address. The task of the Bible student is to learn what actually God has said. Hannah's trouble comes not merely because her husband has another wife, but because that wife has borne children to Elkanah, while Hannah has not had any children. Women who wish for children and do not have them deserve compassion in any culture, but the culture of ancient Israel was particularly hard on such women. Inheritance and the next generation were on the mind of every man, because God's blessings to Abraham had focused on the great nation, the land that was to be handed down from generation to generation, and the coming of a blessing for the entire world from this nation on this land. Elkanah loved his wife, but he was unable to change her problem, and her lack of a son caused her much distress.

Hannah's third problem was that even the priest of God's people did not understand her. He observed her moving her lips without making any sounds, and he assumed that she was drunk. This might be the lowest point at Hannah's life, to be scolded by God's priest while she is praying to God. Yet things change for her on this very day: when she explains her predicament to the priest, he speaks a blessing upon her, and God answers her prayer.

God answered Hannah's prayer not because she prayed it so well, nor because Eli said the magic words to grant her request, but because God is gracious. Hannah's bargain with God did not make Him change His mind; He had already planned what He was going to do before she offered her first son for His service. Samuel would become another in a line of miracle children that stretches from Isaac, the son of Sarah and Abraham, to John, the son of Elizabeth and Zechariah. Each of those miracle children is, in turn, a reminder of Jesus, the Son of Mary, whose birth was the greatest miracle of any child born in the history of God's people.

Hannah's song of joy at the birth of Samuel stands out as a classic hymn, much like the Magnificat of Mary. It is an expression of faith and trust in the Lord. The gift of her son to the service of the Lord is a reminder of the offering of firstfruits that was required from every family of Israel; it also is a picture of God giving His only Son to rescue the world from sin and from death. Hannah continues to care for her son even while he lives in the tabernacle in the service of God, and God the Father continued to care for His Son even while Jesus lived on earth in the service of God's people. Hannah's life was changed by God's grace. No longer was she struggling with problems that distressed her, but she was blessed by God and in turn became a blessing for all God's people.

3 Michal (1 Samuel 18:17–19:17; 2 Samuel 3:12–16; 6:16–23)

Later in the Book of 1 Samuel, we meet another woman who also has to face a difficult situation. Michal is the daughter of King Saul. Very often, the daughter of a king can be useful to his kingdom as a way of rewarding heroes or cementing alliances. This turns out to be the case for Michal. Her father offers her in marriage to David. Most likely, Saul never asked her opinion or permission before making this offer. The king then pressures David into marrying the princess, even though David objects that he is a poor man and has no reputation (1 Samuel 18:23). In fact, Saul's motives are not good in seeking this marriage. He hopes that David will seek to become a greater hero and will die in battle. Instead, David performs greater heroics, and the marriage the king had proposed takes place.

The story of David and Michal could have been a beautiful romance. She was in love with him even before the wedding, and David seems to have been fond of her. Saul's growing hatred of David is a major impediment to the romance of their marriage. Like her brother Jonathan, Michal must choose between loyalty to her father, the king of Israel, and loyalty to her husband, the hero of Israel. Like Jonathan, Michal prefers David to Saul. The king's unreasonable hatred of David and his attacks upon David must have made it difficult for Michal to remain loyal to her father. Instead, because she genuinely loves David, she takes steps to preserve the life of her husband.

When Saul sends messengers to David's house with plans to murder David, Michal helps David escape through a window. Then, at risk to herself, she makes it appear that David is asleep in bed to buy time for his escape. Ironically, she chooses an image—an idol, a false god—to take the place of her husband. Idols were made in ancient times (and in times not so ancient) to represent various gods, and many cultures considered them to be dwelling places of the gods. The true God had told His people to make no idols. Less than two months after God spoke this command from Mount Sinai, and all the people had heard what God said, Aaron, the brother of Moses, broke this command and formed a golden calf for the Israelites to worship. If Michal was able so quickly to find an idol to take the place of her husband (and so save his life), then someone in the household must have been using that idol in place of the true God, the one who would send His Son into the world to take the place of sinners and save us for all eternity.

The heroic deception of Michal saves David's life, but it also begins a long separation between Michal and the husband she loves. David hides in the wilderness in the south of Israel, where he eventually marries other women. Michal is given by her father as a bride to Paltiel (Palti for short), the son of Laish, who was from Gallim (1 Samuel 25:44). After Saul died and his son Ish-bosheth had been assassinated, Abner, the general of Israel's army, returned Michal to David's household, and Paltiel followed after her, mourning, until Abner sent him back home (2 Samuel 3:15–16). From this brief detail, we might guess that Paltiel and Michal must have had a happy marriage. David evidently wanted his first wife back with him more for political reasons than because of affection for her. After she criticized his dance of joy before the ark of the Lord, they were clearly estranged. One noble and courageous act performed by Michal was not enough to grant her lasting happiness, even though it did preserve David's life at a time when he needed help.

4 Abigail (1 Samuel 25; 2 Samuel 3:3)

Abigail was another woman who befriended David and became his wife. However, the circumstances of her relationship with David are very different from those of Michal. For one thing, she was already married to another man when she met David, and he was married to Michal (although they had been separated by now). Abigail was married to a man with the unlikely name of Nabal, which means "fool." In fact, we even see that he lived "up" to the meaning of his name in acting as a fool.

David and his band of outlaws, six hundred strong, were living in the wilderness of Paran. The men kept patrol in the region, not only protecting David from Saul and the army of Israel, but also watching out for bands of Philistines, Amalekites, or other groups that would have been a threat to Israel. Because of the attention of David and his men, the flocks and the workers of Nabal were kept safe. Not even a wild animal stole so much as a single sheep from the flock. At the time for shearing the sheep (which was like a holiday because of the change in routine, and therefore an excuse for parties and feasts), David sent messengers to ask for a share in Nabal's feast. In North America today, such a request might seem presumptuous, and Nabal acted as if it was an unreasonable request to him as well. All the other people involved, though, saw it as a perfectly natural request. David had performed a valuable favor to Nabal over the past few months. Nabal owed him a favor. This time of celebration was as good a time as any for David to make this sort of request.

David is furious when Nabal not only refuses his request but also insults David and his men. At this time, Abigail springs into action. Like Michal, she acts to protect her husband, but we can note a very important difference: Nabal did not deserve such protection, because he had brought danger upon himself. For three reasons, Abigail protects him. First, many innocent people would have suffered along with him in his punishment. Second, David could have come to harm as a result of his revenge upon Nabal. Third, unlike Michal, Abigail deceives no one in the way she protects her husband. Instead, she does the good thing that he should have done in the first place.

David recognizes the wisdom of Abigail and the goodness of her actions. He thanks her and commends her and sends her home, and then he allows God to take vengeance instead of seeking it by his own hands. God does strike Nabal down as Nabal deserves, and David then marries the widow. Not only does he gain all the property that Nabal was so eager to protect and keep to himself, but David also gains a wise and respected wife as well. Unlike Michal, Abigail does bear a son of King David, whose name (according to 2 Samuel 3:3) was Chileab. This son is not as famous as some of the other sons of David. Given the fact that most of those sons are famous for their sins and their mistakes, perhaps the lack of news about Chileab is one more indication of the wisdom and good sense of his mother, Abigail.

5 The Medium of En-dor (1 Samuel 28)

The final famous woman in the Book of 1 Samuel is not known to us by name, but is identified only as a "medium" at En-dor. A medium is a person who attempts to communicate with the spirits of people who have died. In the Law of Moses, such practices are absolutely prohibited. Saul had, during his better days as king of Israel, enforced the Law of Moses and demanded that mediums leave Israel. However, this woman had not left; she had violated the law. Now, no longer faithful to God and no longer blessed by God, Saul violates his own law (which had conformed to God's Law) and visits this medium. He wants to communicate with the spirit of Samuel, since Saul expects to get accurate and helpful information from the ghost of the dead prophet.

A writer of religious fiction would probably have made such a character completely unlikable. As a sinner knowingly violating one of God's most basic commandments by practicing a false religion, this woman would probably have been given no good qualities by the average author. God's Word, however, reports her finer qualities. She is compassionate toward the king and sincerely helpful to him in his time of need. Her fear of being punished as she deserves for breaking the law does not keep her from wanting to help the man who proclaimed that law. The medium from En-dor is a sinner, but she possesses some virtue all the same.

More surprising than her good qualities, though, is the fact that God chooses to work through her to accomplish His plan. God does not want people to sin, but when people do sin, God can work through sinners and even through their sins. Saul wants to speak to the spirit of Samuel, and God allows the spirit of Samuel to appear. The medium's surprise at seeing Samuel appear has led many readers of the Bible to assume that her "visitations" were usually the result of fraud. Of course, we know that the spirits of the dead do not return to the earth; those who die trusting God's promises wait in paradise for Resurrection Day, while those who die outside of the faith are imprisoned in Hades until Judgment Day. Still, some people sincerely believe that they can communicate with the spirits of the dead. Whether they are misled by demons or by their own imaginations, they expect to hear from spirits and are not surprised when they receive an answer. Hence, this medium's surprise when Samuel appears may be a hint about the quality of her usual séances.

God in no way condones Saul's use of a medium or the practice of calling upon the dead. Nevertheless, God works through this sinful situation instigated by Saul. Through it, Saul is told what he needs to know. We are comforted to know that God works through us sinners and our sinful actions. We have all sinned and fallen short of God's perfect plan for our lives. Christ, through His death, still works in us and through us to bring about His plan.

Conclusion

Throughout the Book of 1 Samuel, women are seen as heroic, no less than the men. We can always recall and give thanks for the sacrifices made and risks taken by all of these women; even, to a certain extent, the medium of En-dor. No less than Abigail or Michal, this woman took a risk in order to be helpful to a person in need. Christ's sacrifice on the cross is dimly pictured in the sacrifices of these women, just as it can be seen in the risks and sacrifices that heroic men and women make in various situations throughout history all over the world. All such self-sacrificial actions, words, and attitudes are reflections of that great act of compassion when our Lord Jesus sacrificed Himself for us at Golgotha.

Christians, of course, are called to imitate Christ—to live lives in a self-sacrificial manner for the benefit of others. However, while we know that we cannot save the world by our own sacrifices, still and all, we know that we can help others through such acts of love. True, love does make one vulnerable, because love always involves the risk of sacrifice. Since we are called to love our neighbors as ourselves, we know that at times we will have to make sacrifices or even take risks for others. At times, we can see that even those outside the faith can become reminders of Christ and of Christlike living. Then we are encouraged all the more to be like Christ ourselves, loving and serving others rather than thinking only about ourselves.

Nevertheless, we can certainly remember that the sacrifice of Christ is unique—truly and even eternally unique. Although other peoples' sacrificial acts may bring Jesus' sacrifice to mind, Christ is the only sinless victim who can atone for the world's sins. Our own sacrificial acts, like those of the women in 1 Samuel, find their greatest significance in being reflections and reminders of that eternal sacrifice of the Son of God.

Concluding Activities

Speak a closing prayer, make any necessary announcements, and distribute study leaflet 6.

The King Is Dead! Long Live the King!

2 Samuel 1–6

Preparing for the Session

Central Focus

Every king, even a bad king, is a picture of Jesus, the King of kings.

Objectives

That participants, led by the Holy Spirit working through God's Word, will

1. recognize and imitate David's respect for those in authority;
2. exercise their own authority over others responsibly, remembering Jesus Christ, the source of all authority; and
3. honor Jesus as King of kings and Lord of lords.

Note for the small-group leaders: Lesson notes and other materials you will need begin on page 61.

For the Lecture Leader

Session Plan

Worship

Begin the session with the hymn printed in the study leaflet. Accompaniments are available in denominational hymnals, such as *Lutheran Service Book* or *Lutheran Worship*. (Note: Concordia Publishing House has available *The Concordia Organist*. All the initial worship hymns in the LifeLight courses are included in this resource. It's especially helpful for mission congregations and small parishes. See the list of study resources on page 7.) Follow with this prayer:

Prayer

Jesus, Son of God and Son of David, we honor You as King of kings and Lord of lords. Help us to remember that Your authority in our lives comes not only through the Means of Grace and the work of the Church, but also through human government. Through the work of Your Holy Spirit, teach us to respect those who have authority over us, to use the authority given to us responsibly, and to show our love for You in the way we love our leaders. We pray this in Your name, Jesus, our King and Lord. Amen.

Lecture Presentation

1 Introduction

As the old saying goes, "patience is a virtue." And patience, like most virtues, is often most noted for its absence rather than its presence. This was very likely the case with David's troops. One can only imagine that, occasionally, the men of David's fighting force must have lost their patience with him. He could be most exasperating at times! From his men's point of view, there is probably no other way to say it.

There were times when David's actions and behavior seemed precisely counter to the best interests of him and his followers. For instance, while being pursued by King Saul, David twice had the advantage when he could have killed Saul, ended the pursuit, and hastened the day when he could claim the kingdom. Yet, both times, he allowed Saul to escape, and he even signaled to the king and told him of the situation, making it harder for David's men to hope for a future plan to overthrow King Saul. Why in the world did he do this? What would have led David to treat Saul, his enemy, in this manner?

2 Respect for Authority (2 Samuel 1–4)

David's actions were likely exasperating to his men, and at times they may seem confusing to us—the opposite of what we would expect. We cannot help but notice that when Saul died in battle, David did not rejoice. Instead of being overjoyed by the news, he openly mourned for King Saul and for Prince Jonathan. And then David did not appear at all interested in making use of the open throne to advance his own claim to the kingdom. Instead, he seemed quite content to allow other people to make other plans. Even more startling, the man who brought news to David of Saul's death was executed by David for having claimed to have killed the king. Apparently, the messenger had assumed that he was bringing good news and would be rewarded. His "reward" was not at all what he had expected. The messenger did not realize that David would be so vengeful against the one who claimed to have killed Saul.

Then David stood by and did nothing as Saul's son Ish-bosheth was made king of Israel. To many people, this probably made no sense at all. We know that David already had been declared king of Judah, and war was fought between the two parts of the divided kingdom. In spite of this war, and in spite of the fact that Samuel had anointed David king over all of Israel, David was not glad when he heard that Ish-bosheth was killed. David executed the assassins of Ish-bosheth and publicly denounced what they had done. Even though their work made David king of all twelve tribes, he still treated them as murderers, not national heroes.

David's respect for the authority of Saul seems almost obsessive, but David had good reasons to honor the king. First, clearly David remembered the Ten Commandments, which God had given His people through Moses. David understood that the Commandment "Honor your father and your mother" (Exodus 20:12), applies not only to the household but also to other relationships of worldly authority. As the apostle Paul wrote to the Christians in Rome, (Romans 13:1) "Let every person be subject to the governing authorities. For there is no authority except from God, and those that exist have been instituted by God." The next six verses of Romans 13 speak to this as well. Peter also applied this Commandment this way: (1 Peter 2:13–14) "Be subject for the Lord's sake to every human institution, whether it be to the emperor as supreme, or to governors as sent by him." God, through the writers of the Bible, demanded obedience and respect to human governments, and David modeled that obedience and respect in some very vivid ways.

The Commandment continues, (Exodus 20:12) "Honor your father and your mother, that your days may be long in the land that the Lord your God is giving you." Respect for authority and obedience to its laws strengthen a nation. When citizens honor, respect, and obey their leaders—not in the sense of placing them over God, but rather serving them under God—then the work of those leaders is made easier and the nation prospers. However, when citizens mock and scorn their leaders and challenge their right to rule, the work of those leaders is made more difficult, and as a result, the nation suffers.

If, as Paul writes in the Book of Romans, all authority comes from God, then one of the ways in which people show their regard for God is in the way they treat human authority. In other words, those who challenge human authority challenge God, but those who submit to human authority submit to God. Here we see that David continued to respect Saul even when David had to run away and hide from him. David would not rejoice publicly at the deaths of Saul and Ish-bosheth because doing so would insult the memory of those who had held authority over David and over all the people of Israel.

3 Respect for the Office (2 Samuel 1–4)

The example David set in his respect for Saul's authority was probably one he intended others to follow later, once he became king. If David had mocked Saul, either before or after Saul died, others might have felt free to mock David as king. If David had participated in the overthrow of Saul or the assassination of Ish-bosheth, people might have felt free to remove David from the throne in the same manner. And, of course, David knew that there was no reason for him to even consider following such a course. David knew that, already as a boy, he had been chosen by God as king of Israel. He was willing to be patient and to allow the throne to come to him according to God's schedule and in peaceful ways, rather than seizing for himself what God already had promised to bestow upon him.

Therefore, David punished the man who claimed to have killed Saul, as well as those who murdered Ish-bosheth. David also refused to show any disrespect for Abner, Saul's general, when he was murdered. Even though he is remembered as a mighty warrior king, David deplored unnecessary violence. He wanted what was best for Israel, not merely what was best for his own career. By putting the land ahead of himself and by putting the office of king ahead of his own ambition to be king, David set a worthy example for the citizens of both ancient Israel and the world's countries today.

Unfortunately, it is an example that is so often ignored. We can see examples of this so frequently. Entertainers mock those in authority, knowing that they will easily gain the approval of their audiences with this sort of humor. Candidates who want to win elections often assume that the quickest path to victory is to scorn and speak disparagingly of the incumbent. This lack of respect for authority filters down through society, affecting relationships in families and schools and workplaces. Things are not peaceful in the land, precisely because respect for authority at every level has been eroded. Temptations from the devil and from the world to despise those in authority are met with glee by our sinful nature, which loves to tear down others so we can feel better about ourselves.

And yet, through it all, we may not think anything at all of wallowing in such lack of respect for authority—it is so common that it just seems like a normal part of life—why should it ever concern us? However, we can recall what we just said about the commandment to "honor your father and your mother": in our disregarding the human authorities that God has established over us in our life, we are also doing something even more serious. For in this way, we show God how we truly feel, in our sin-stained hearts, about His authority over our lives.

4 Respect for the Future King (2 Samuel 1–4)

The picture that we see of David here in 2 Samuel stands in stark contrast to that. David, the man who would be king, demonstrated his loyalty and respect to those who were king before him. Let's be clear about what that was all about. It would be a mistake to think that David's behavior was simply a cynical display he put on to reinforce his own future authority. No, it was far more than that.

David looked beyond himself to the one who would sit on the throne of Israel after him, the Son of David who would rule an eternal kingdom. David had not yet been told that his descendant would be the Chosen One of Israel, but David knew that such a king was coming. From the writings of Moses, David knew that God had in mind a great king to come from His people, an Anointed One who would do more than rule over twelve tribes in the Jordan River valley. This is precisely why David spoke of Saul as the Lord's anointed and refused to raise his hand against Saul: because David regarded Saul as a picture and a reminder of the greater Anointed One who was yet to come. What this means is that David's loyalty to Saul and his respect for Saul was, in truth, a display of David's loyalty to Jesus and respect for Jesus.

By allowing himself (the next anointed king of Israel) to be subject to Saul (the current anointed king of Israel), David himself acts as a picture and a reminder of Jesus. Like David, Jesus is the true King of the Jews, and not only of the Jews, but of all people. Yet Jesus did not assert His authority against the earthly authorities ruling in Galilee and Judea when He was visibly on earth. Jesus did not work to overthrow the authority of the Roman governor, nor did He preach an uprising against the priests in the temple, corrupt though they were. Jesus instead modeled respect for authority. He paid His taxes and urged others to pay their taxes. Even when He was arrested and falsely accused, He did not defy the authority of those who tried Him. They abused their authority in the way they treated Him, but Jesus accepted their authority over Him, going to the cross to pay for their sins and for the sins of the entire world.

We can recall Jesus saying to Roman governor Pontius Pilate, (John 18:36) "My kingdom is not from the world." However, many Jews at that time wanted a Messiah who would claim a worldly kingdom. They wanted a Messiah who would reestablish the throne of David, rule in Jerusalem, and dominate the surrounding nations. Worldly domination—that is an enticing thought. Even today, many followers of Jesus want His kingdom to take this kind of worldly authority, telling governments how to rule their people and making laws to enforce the Law of God.

How should we consider such opinions? We can certainly agree with these people to a degree. After all, ideally, the rules and regulations of human government should conform to the unchanging truth of God's Word. Ideally, Christian citizens should take their part in the democracies of the world and work for better government on earth while waiting for the kingdom of God to be fully revealed when Jesus appears in glory. None of that can be denied. However, we should not deceive ourselves. Jesus was not lying to the governor when He said, "My kingdom is not from the world." He did not establish a Church on earth so that it could rule with human authority. Rather, He established a Church on earth so that it could share the Gospel, bringing forgiveness to sinners and granting eternal life to those whose disobedience to God's commands had brought them to death.

5 Joy in Zion (2 Samuel 5–6)

Samuel had feared the consequences of linking too closely the political structure of Israel with the authority of God and His Word. He was concerned that such a close association between God and king could lead to the king grossly abusing his authority. However, David's honor for Saul and for the coming Messiah reduced the danger that he would abuse the Israelites in the manner in which Samuel had threatened. David did become king of Israel. He ruled over Judah for seven years and then over all twelve tribes for another thirty-three years.

He captured Jerusalem from the Jebusites and made it his capital city. He built a palace there on Mount Zion, so that from that time on, people would associate Zion with the rule of David and his descendants (even with the promised Messiah, the Son of David) and would call the government of Israel "Zion," they same way that Americans speak of their government as "Washington."

King David also brought the ark of the covenant into Jerusalem. This gave Jerusalem far greater significance than merely being a capital city. We can recall what a great and tremendous thing the ark of the covenant was. This was the chest that contained the mementos reminding the Israelites of God's grace and mercy to their forefathers. It contained the tablets of the Law, a pot of manna, and Aaron's rod that had budded. But even more than being a symbol or reminder, the ark was the place where the people were to turn to continue to receive the grace of God then. For on top of the ark was the mercy seat, and above this seat was where God had chosen to dwell in the midst of His people. The presence of the ark in Jerusalem meant that not only was the city David's capital, but that God's gracious presence was also there with them always.

Moving the ark to Jerusalem was not so easily accomplished. When he first tried to move the ark, David chose a form of transportation that seemed right to him, having it pulled in a cart by oxen. This mistake resulted in a tragic death. Later, David must have returned to the writings of Moses to learn how the ark was meant to be moved, because on its second journey under his orders, the ark was carried on poles by priests as God had commanded (Exodus 25:14). As hard as he tried to obey all the Lord's commands, David was not without sin or error. Doing things his way before he studied to learn God's way was a mistake, and another man paid the price for David's mistake.

When the ark finally arrived in Jerusalem, David danced for joy before this visible reminder of the presence of the Lord. This dance was not commanded by God, but neither was it forbidden by God. It reflected David's own joy that God's visible presence would remain in the capital city of David's kingdom. The ark, like the sacrifices, brought good news to God's people. It spoke of the fact that God dwelt in the midst of His people, claiming them and removing their guilt and shame. No other god did that. The ark, like the sacrifices, was a picture of Jesus, the greater King of God's people. David's dance before the ark humbled him, but he was humbled for the greater glory of his God and Savior.

David's wife Michal, the daughter of King Saul, disapproved of the dance of David. She may not have been opposed to dancing in all circumstances, but she did not like to see the king of Israel—her husband!—humble himself in public. She spoke scornfully to David about his dancing, but in the end it was she who was humbled and not David. King David was willing to humble himself in the presence of a reminder of the greater King who was yet to come. And so, in spite of Michal's objection, it was fitting rather than demeaning that David humbled himself on this occasion.

Conclusion

Our reading this week has dealt with the authority of kings. But, of course, we know that what we see exemplified here is not limited to just kingly or governmental authority, but extends to all legitimate earthly authorities. This makes the relation between David and Saul a significant one for us, because we know that many people have authority in this world. Parents have authority at home, business owners and managers have authority in the workplace, teachers have authority in classrooms, pastors and other leaders have authority in congregations, and various government officials have authority at all levels of government. Just as David owed Saul his respect because Saul was king, we know that those who have earthly authority over us deserve our respect and honor. They can expect our obedience, except in those matters where they demand that God's people break God's commands. They deserve this honor and obedience because their authority comes from God Himself and because they are, in a sense, images of God and His rule over the universe.

Yet with power comes responsibility. Those who exercise authority are expected to do so for the good of others, not merely for their own benefit. Those who exercise authority are expected to do their jobs carefully and wisely, not taking for granted the privileges that come with authority. Those who exercise authority are expected to do so humbly, remembering that greater authority who has granted them the right to rule. David's respect for King Saul and his dance before the ark of the Lord exhibit both sides of this definition of power.

Concluding Activities

Speak a closing prayer, make any necessary announcements, and distribute study leaflet 7.

You Are the Man!

2 Samuel 7–12

Preparing for the Session

Central Focus

As David sinned, repented, and was absolved, so also sinners today fall short of God's plan, cannot save themselves by what they do, but are redeemed by Christ.

Objectives

That participants, led by the Holy Spirit working through God's Word, will

1. identify the high cost of sin;
2. identify Jesus as the Redeemer who pays for the sins of the world; and
3. confess their sins and be confident of God's forgiveness through Christ.

Note for the small-group leaders: Lesson notes and other materials you will need begin on page 63.

For the Lecture Leader

Session Plan

Worship

Begin the session with the hymn printed in the study leaflet. Accompaniments are available in denominational hymnals, such as *Lutheran Service Book* or *Lutheran Worship*. (Note: Concordia Publishing House has available *The Concordia Organist*. All the initial worship hymns in the LifeLight courses are included in this resource. It's especially helpful for mission congregations and small parishes. See the list of study resources on page 7.) Follow with this prayer:

Prayer

Holy God, heavenly Father, have mercy on us according to Your steadfast love. According to Your abundant mercy, blot out our transgressions. Wash us thoroughly from our iniquity, and cleanse us from our sins. Hide Your face from all our sins, and blot out all our iniquities. Create in us clean hearts, and renew in us right spirits. All this we ask in the name of Your Son, our Savior, Jesus Christ. Amen.

Lecture Presentation

1 Introduction

What if you had to tell the king that he was wrong? Certainly, that would not be an enviable position to be in. Kings generally do not like to be contradicted, especially not in public. They have ways of winning arguments that are not available to folk without a crown. We can remember, for example, that when John the Baptist spoke publicly against the sins of the tetrarch Herod, son of Herod the Great, John was arrested and later beheaded for his preaching. There have been others throughout history. Thomas Becket, for instance, suffered a similar fate for his opposition to King Henry II of England. And certainly, long before the martyrdoms of John and Thomas, wise men already knew that it was dangerous to accuse the king.

Yet, that is exactly what we find here in 2 Samuel 12. When Nathan the prophet was sent by God to warn King David of his sin, Nathan came prepared with an eloquent speech. He describes a situation in which a man of wealth and power abuses these blessings for his own benefit and to the harm of his poorer neighbor. The story is sufficiently removed from the details of David's sin that the king is slow to see the point of the story. (Vv. 6–7) "The man who has done this deserves to die," the king thunders from his throne of judgment. "You are the man!" Nathan replies. David stands judged and condemned in his own courtroom, because the sins of which he is guilty surpass those that inspired his anger.

2 God Condemns Sin (2 Samuel 11–12)

What was so bad about David's sins? At first blush, it might not seem so terrible. He loved a woman and slept with her, although she was not his wife. For many people, this would be no great concern. After all, such people might reason, if they were two consenting adults, then why not approve of their behavior, or at least ignore it and let them live their own lives? Many books and movies feature men like David and women like Bathsheba, and few of those books and movies ever condemn their characters for being in love and expressing their love to each other.

However, such an opinion would be overlooking something rather significant. God has always treated adultery as a more serious matter than many people do, and God's Word speaks strongly against adultery in a way that many books and movies do not. One reason for God's severe attitude toward this sin is that it is rarely a victimless crime. Absent spouses are hurt by the sin of adultery, regardless of whether they know it is happening. Children of the families involved are hurt by their parents' sin. Even the two people who thought they were in love and were doing nothing wrong frequently come to regret their mistake and feel in their own lives the pain they have caused by their sinful behavior.

A second reason God condemns adultery is that the love of husband and wife is a picture of His love for His people. God provides the gift of marriage for several reasons—for mutual support, as a foundation for families, and as a structure for society, for example. Foremost among God's reasons to value marriage highly is that every marriage is a picture of Christ and His love for the Church. We see this very vividly explained by St. Paul in Ephesians 5. After discussing marriage, Paul concludes by writing, (vv. 31–32) "'Therefore a man shall leave his father and mother and hold fast to his wife, and the two shall become one flesh.' This mystery is profound, and I am saying that it refers to Christ and the church." And this comparison is not unique to the New Testament; Old Testament Israel was frequently described by Moses and the prophets as God's Bride. When Israel turned to false gods, this sin was characterized as adultery. Deliberate destruction of a marriage is rejection of God's gift of love; it is an insult to God Himself. Therefore, God does not approve even of fictions and fantasies that rely on adultery to be entertaining.

Yet we know that temptations come to all people. Even Jesus was tempted, though He was without sin. David was tempted when he saw Bathsheba from his palace roof. In a similar manner, Joseph the son of Jacob was also tempted in Egypt when his master's wife invited him to commit adultery with her. It would have been easy for Joseph to say yes to temptation. The two of them might have gratified their desires, and no one else might ever have known what they had done. Joseph's answer, though, remains the classic right answer to temptation: (Genesis 39:9) "How then can I do this great wickedness and sin against God?" Though it would have been easy to say yes to this temptation, Joseph found a very good reason to say no instead.

David's adultery is even worse, though, because he is the king of Israel. He has a high standard to uphold as the earthly ruler of God's people. Whenever a man of power in the world draws a woman into adultery, he is abusing his power over her. This is true even if she seeks or encourages his attention. David's adultery with Bathsheba is an abuse of his power as king of Israel, which means that David has sinned against his nation as well as against Bathsheba, her husband, and God.

We could look at it as several sins all rolled up into one. This is not unusual. Sins rarely come singly, and David's adultery is part of an entire web of sins. His sin begins with coveting his neighbor's wife, continues with the act of adultery, and then leads to a growing collection of lies and deceit as he tries to hide the consequences. Uriah is called home from the battlefield, with David hoping that he will spend an evening with his wife and appear to be the father of the child that is expected. When Uriah does not follow David's script, David resorts to murder (hidden in further lies) to get rid of Uriah. Then he tries to deceive the nation by marrying his officer's widow, becoming the widow's caretaker without confessing the many sins that had made her a widow expecting a child.

Coveting, false witness, adultery, and murder are all clearly and absolutely forbidden by God's commandments. As the prophet Nathan reminds David, though, an additional sin belongs at the head of the list. David has despised God and God's gifts to David by claiming for himself someone who belonged to another. Beginning with when David saw Uriah's wife on the rooftop and coveted her, he was sinning against God, convincing himself that God had not provided him with everything that was good for him and right for him to have. Had David remembered Joseph's answer to temptation, he could have resisted, but instead he used his power as king to take what God had not given him or offered to him.

If David had been more like the tetrarch Herod or King Henry II of England, then Nathan would have been in danger for reminding David of his sins. Instead, David confessed that he was wrong, saying, (2 Samuel 12:13) "I have sinned against the Lord." Nathan had the privilege, after warning David of his sin, of absolving David, saying, "The Lord also has put away your sin; you shall not die." In spite of this absolution, Nathan proceeds to warn David that his sin will have earthly consequences, not only for himself but for other people as well.

3 Grace, and the Consequences of Sin (2 Samuel 12)

This blend of forgiveness and warning of continued consequences can be hard for us to understand. Some people use this episode as proof that God really is angry and vengeful, reaching out in anger to bring death and sorrow whenever His rules are not obeyed. This interpretation is not consistent with the Bible's message of God, who is a God of love and mercy and grace. Others see the death of the baby as a reminder that sin has results, even when it is forgiven. The wages of sin is death, and David cannot be allowed to escape his sins without any reaction from God, even if David has repented and been absolved by the prophet and forgiven by God. We must not take sin lightly, they remind us, because even forgiven sins still have consequences in this sinful world. God's people ought to take care always to avoid temptation and sin.

Still other people see the death of this son of David as a reminder of Christ, the future Son of David who will also die to pay for David's sins, and for the sins of all the world. Both were innocent of the sins that led to their deaths, but both rescued David by taking on themselves the death he deserved. The irony concerning this earlier son of David is that he would never have lived at all if David had not sinned. Had David been aware that the baby would die, he might not have taken such drastic actions to hide his sin, murdering Uriah so he could marry Bathsheba.

Regardless, David is to be commended for his concern for the baby, even when he has been told that the baby will die. David prays and fasts and seeks mercy for his son; he does not stop to think that, if this baby had never existed, his sin would never have been revealed and compounded by further sins. David knows that it is unfair that another person should die so he can live, and he seeks to overturn the verdict. When the baby does die, though, David ceases his mourning. (2 Samuel 12:23) "I shall go to him," David says, "but he will not return to me."

There is something here that is so deeply comforting. In all of his prayers for the baby, one thing is evident: David is convinced of the graciousness and goodness of the Lord. David's confidence in the grace of God is so strong that he is confident of the salvation even of this uncircumcised boy. Grieving parents of stillborn children have found comfort in the confidence of David that the families of God's people will be reunited on God's schedule. We cannot bring back to life those who have died, but God has promised a resurrection to eternal life for all those who belong to Him.

4 You Are *Not* the Man! (2 Samuel 7)

David was covered by the grace and mercy of God throughout his life, even when he sinned by coveting and committing adultery and lying and murdering. The death of the Son of God, roughly a thousand years in David's future, was sufficient to pay the price for all of David's sins. When David wanted to hide his sins, God sent the prophet Nathan to confront David with the words "You are the man!" On the other hand, when David wanted to do something good for God, the same prophet was sent to tell David, "You are not the man!"

When David brought the ark of God into Jerusalem, he danced for joy in its presence. Some years later, David was struck by the fact that he was living in a palace, while the visible reminder of God's presence in the midst of His people was still being kept in a tent. When David told Nathan that he was going to build a temple to be the house of the Lord in Jerusalem, Nathan at first spoke words of approval. But that night, God spoke to the prophet in a dream. Nathan was to tell David that he, David, would not build a house for God, but that God would make David a house (2 Samuel 7:11). In this vision, God told Nathan to promise David many blessings: He would make David famous, He would establish Israel in peace and security, and they would be safe from all their enemies. Greatest of all these blessings, though, was the promised Son of David, the one who would build a house for God and would rule an eternal kingdom. He would be not only the Son of David, but also the Son of God. He would be disciplined for sin, but would not eternally lose the love of God. Instead, He would rule forever in the name of His father David.

5 Solomon and Jesus (2 Samuel 7)

We cannot know how completely David understood this promise of a Son who would rule an eternal kingdom. At times, David seems to have been convinced that Solomon was the promised son who would build God a house. David made plans for the temple of the Lord, purchased the land, arranged for the materials, and handed all this over to Solomon so that the temple could be built in Jerusalem. In many ways, David seemed to regard Solomon as the fulfillment of God's promise. Of course, we know that Solomon failed to be the perfect Son of David. He sinned, building temples to false gods and worshiping in them as well as in the temple of the true God. Solomon, in fact, did all the things that Samuel warned the Israelites that a king would do to them.

Of course, as it turned out, Solomon did not rule an eternal kingdom. Like his father, David, he died. After his death, Israel split into two kingdoms. Both were eventually conquered by empires from the east. God's people had to wait a thousand tumultuous years for the promised Son of David to be born. But though they had to wait, the promises of God were sure and certain and, at God's appointed time, came to fulfillment.

The Son of David, the one would came to be our eternal King, was born in Bethlehem, the city of David. He lived among God's people, much as the ark had been among God's people to remind them of God's presence. He was more than a symbol, though; He was the real presence of God in the midst of His people. Jesus even identified Himself with the temple in Jerusalem, saying, (John 2:19) "Destroy this temple, and in three days I will raise it up." John reminds us further, (v. 21) "He was speaking about the temple of His body." The body of Jesus was truly a temple, since God Himself was dwelling there.

Even though Jesus never sinned, God the Father treated Him as guilty of the world's sins and allowed Him to be punished for that guilt. In bearing our the guilt of all our sins, the sinless One then became the greatest sinner of all, for all of our guilt before God was laid upon Him. As the prophet Isaiah explains, (53:5) "He was pierced for our transgressions; He was crushed for our iniquities; upon Him was the chastisement that brought us peace, and with His wounds we are healed." From this, we understand what God told Nathan to tell David about the Son of David: (2 Samuel 7:14) "When He commits iniquity, I will discipline Him with the rod of men, with the stripes of the son of men." Jesus was seen as guilty—as sin itself—so David and other sinners, you and I included, could be innocent in the sight of God. The innocent One assumed our guilt so that we who were guilty would be viewed by God as innocent forever.

Jesus died as payment for all those sins, but He did not remain dead. Death could not keep Him, the grave could not hold Him, for our sins had not defeated Him. On the third day, He rose again to prove His victory over death and the grave and to share that victory with all who trust in Him. His death and resurrection are the foundation of His kingdom, a kingdom that is truly eternal. Before they were expelled from Eden, Adam and Eve were told that their descendant would triumph over Satan. Later on, the promise was repeated when Abraham was told that from his family living in the Promised Land would come a blessing for the entire world. And then again, God repeated this promise when David was told that his Son would rule an eternal kingdom. All those who heard and believed these promises are members of His eternal kingdom. All those who hear and believe them today are members of His eternal kingdom.

Conclusion

David was the man who sinned against God and deserved to die. David was not the man to build a house for God, even though God was blessing David richly. We also are helpless to earn God's blessings, but we are invited to receive them freely by His grace. David's prayer of confession, preserved in the Bible as Psalm 51, includes this beautiful petition for grace and mercy: (vv. 9–10) "Hide Your face from my sins, and blot out all my iniquities. Create in me a clean heart, O God, and renew a right spirit within me." This prayer God heard and answered.

David no longer was the man who deserved to die, but he was the man who would live in an eternal kingdom, serving the Son who would come from his family and would be the eternal King. Likewise, we know that we, too, deserve nothing but God's wrath and punishment for our sins. We, too, know that, as David prayed in Psalm 51, God has every right to cast us forever from His presence. And yet, thanks be to God, like David, we know that through that eternal Son of David, our Lord Christ, we are forgiven and cleansed by God and are united with Him throughout our lives, and even forever. To the Son of David be glory and honor and praise forever! Amen.

Concluding Activities

Speak a closing prayer, make any necessary announcements, and distribute study leaflet 8.

Absalom, O Absalom

2 Samuel 13–19

Preparing for the Session

Central Focus

A rebellious son who dies in battle becomes a picture of God's sinless Son who dies to pay for the world's rebellion.

Objectives

That participants, led by the Holy Spirit working through God's Word, will

1. recognize the sins of Absalom;
2. perceive how Absalom the son of David can, in spite of his sins, be a picture of Jesus Christ the Son of David; and
3. find their own sins and rebellion crucified with Christ and buried with Him.

Note for the small-group leaders: Lesson notes and other materials you will need begin on page 65.

For the Lecture Leader

Session Plan

Worship

Begin the session with the hymn printed in the study leaflet. Accompaniments are available in denominational hymnals, such as *Lutheran Service Book* or *Lutheran Worship*. (Note: Concordia Publishing House has available *The Concordia Organist*. All the initial worship hymns in the LifeLight courses are included in this resource. It's especially helpful for mission congregations and small parishes. See the list of study resources on page 7.) Follow with this prayer:

Prayer

Lord Jesus Christ, You take away the sins of the world. Grant us joy and peace in our redemption, and help us to see pictures of Your sacrifice and Your victory even in the lives of sinners such as Absalom and David. Amen.

Lecture Presentation

1 Introduction

The third quarter of 2 Samuel describes a family that is falling apart. Though they are the royal family of Israel, God's chosen people, they are still subject to a string of shocking and shameful sins. In short order, the reader witnesses rape, murder, defiance, conspiracy, and open war. It is hard for us to imagine all of the conflict that was inflicted by and upon this one family. Even in television and the movies, it is hard to find this much drama and horror in one family. Ultimately, the troubles of the family are all traced back to David.

It can be difficult to read this account in 2 Samuel and think of all the things David could have done to nip these troubles in the bud. But we see that David could not bring himself to do those things. He loved his family; he loved his sons. He could not bring himself to deal with them harshly. And yet, in the face of his sons' offenses, his gentleness only seemed to encourage more sinfulness.

2 Visiting the Iniquity (2 Samuel 13)

When the prophet Nathan preached against the sins David had committed with Bathsheba, the wife of Uriah—his coveting, their adultery, and the false witness and murder that followed—Nathan prophesied, (2 Samuel 12: 10, 11) "The sword shall never depart from your house. . . . I will raise up evil against you out of your own house."

These two warnings, with the others that accompanied them, are all fulfilled in the following chapters of 2 Samuel. David suffers in all the ways that the prophet described, because he had sinned against the Lord and had taken what did not belong to him.

The sins of his children that hurt David so badly can be seen as the natural results of his own sin with Bathsheba. Coveting and adultery and murder began the pattern in one generation and continued in the next; as God had said at Mount Sinai, (Exodus 20:5) "I the Lord your God am a jealous God, visiting the iniquity of the fathers on the children to the third and fourth generation of those who hate Me." Not just in the family of David, but also today, this is something we can often observe in the world around us. Sin tends to linger in families, sometimes as a genetic disposition to certain temptations, and sometimes as learned behavior, but probably a combination of both causes. How can a father like David say to his children, "Don't make the same mistakes I made"? Even when the words are said, the example speaks louder than the words to the children who see the sins of their parents.

David's sins are not limited to a time of weakness with Bathsheba. David falls short in many ways, leading his family deeper into sin. He does not teach his children respect for the rules and for other people. Perhaps his excuse was that he was too busy fighting wars and ruling the kingdom, but David raises two sons who think that rules do not apply to them. They do what they want and do not even care that their sins hurt other people. David compounds this first mistake by not responding appropriately when his sons sin. He was angry when he heard of the rape of Tamar, but he did nothing to punish Amnon. When Absalom murdered Amnon, he fled before he could be punished, and later he was allowed to return to Jerusalem without suffering any consequences for the murder.

Their sins had no apparent consequences; their crimes no sure and certain punishments. Although David clearly loved his sons, his indulgence of their transgressions caused tremendous harm. Rather than rebuking and disciplining them to turn them from their offenses to repentance, David's soft treatment entrenched them in their sinfulness. It helped to harden them in their offenses and actually encouraged further sinfulness. No wonder Absalom believed that the kingdom was his to take, when his father the king was too weak a man to punish the crimes of his own children. Often, conflict occurs because it has been provoked. As it turned out, David's display of weakness was all the provocation that Absalom needed.

3 Civil War (2 Samuel 14:1–15:12)

The result of all this sin was war within Israel. A civil war is always the cruelest kind of war, and this war was especially cruel, because it pitted a father against his own son. How could the soldiers be expected to choose between their king and his heir? How could the nation know which king to follow? In some ways, this civil war between David and Absalom was even more dreadful than the war that followed the death of Solomon, when Jeroboam claimed ten tribes of Israel and left Rehoboam with only two. True, Jeroboam's revolt succeeded, while Absalom's failed, but the turmoil in Israel during Absalom's rebellion was probably worse.

Absalom's scheme for revolution is clever and effective. First, he has prominent people speak on his behalf so that he is permitted to return to Jerusalem. Then, after two years, he arranges to have himself welcomed into King David's presence so he can be accepted by the king, and therefore by everyone else in the government. After this, he makes many public appearances, making himself known to the people of the city and to all those who visit Jerusalem from the twelve tribes of Israel. Especially, he spends time with the people who need government help. His frequent refrain to them is (2 Samuel 15:4) "Oh that I were judge in the land! Then every man with a dispute or cause might come to me, and I would give him justice." This political campaign was very effective, making himself a viable replacement for his father in the eyes of the people, even while David was still alive and in charge of the government.

Above all else, Absalom is particularly clever in suggesting that justice is not being done in Israel. People are always ready to suspect that they are not being treated fairly by the government. Absalom is a talented politician who knows how to use this common trait to his advantage. It does not bother him that he is stealing the kingdom from his father. It does not bother him that he is insulting his father and undermining his authority and rule. Absalom knows what he wants, and he knows how to be patient and skillful in developing a situation that will bring him exactly what he wants.

He also knows how to choose and seize on the best possible moment for his own agenda. When he goes to Hebron and has himself crowned king, the nation is prepared to follow him. People who should know better have allowed themselves to believe that David is not doing his job as king and that Absalom is the right man to replace him. David has no choice but to flee Jerusalem, for if he tries to remain in the capital city and fight his son from there, he risks a bloody civil war that very easily might turn against him.

4 David Flees (2 Samuel 15:13–18:5)

Therefore David flees. Earlier in his life, he had to hide in the wilderness from King Saul, who sought to destroy him. Now he must hide from a false king, his own son

Absalom, who seeks to overthrow him. David's escape from Jerusalem, and the various people who relate to him in a variety of ways on this occasion, make a fascinating study in politics, leadership, and the nature of human beings. At the center, though, remains David, a king who wants to rule his land, but also a father who wants to love his son.

David's mixed feelings about his son Absalom complicate the situation for everyone else. Once again, David falls victim to his tendency to be indulgent of his son's transgressions. Not only has David's lack of fortitude toward his son led his kingdom into a civil war, but now it also threatens to complicate and prolong the conflict. Surely, David could have followed a more decisive course, one way or the other. For example, if David had been willing to abdicate and to give the kingdom to Absalom, all David's followers would have known what to do. Most of them would probably have been unhappy with his choice; some would have protested, and a few might have continued fighting against Absalom.

David does not abdicate, though. He knows that Absalom is not the right man to rule the kingdom of Israel, and David is not prepared to surrender the kingdom to someone who is unfit to rule, even if that man is David's son. On the other hand, if David had responded with righteous anger and wrathful justice, his officers would have known what to do. If David had said, "Strike down and kill that rebel," no soldier in the army would have had any doubt or any hesitation. Those who were going to support Absalom had already left to support him. The rest of the army was prepared to fight against him.

But David does not follow either of these courses. Instead, he seems to vacillate a bit and makes the mission of his army more difficult than perhaps it needs to be. David told his officers and the soldiers, (2 Samuel 18:5) "Deal gently for my sake with the young man Absalom." In his soft-hearted compassion, David makes the job of his army much harder than it would have been otherwise. Consider the mission they have been given: They are asked to seize the kingdom back from Absalom and to defeat his army, but still to deal gently with the chief rebel. All the troops heard David's command; they had no choice but to try to obey the order of their king.

5 Grief and Joy (2 Samuel 18:6–19:43)

The battle is fought, and David's loyal troops overcome the rebel soldiers of Absalom. The rebel chief himself is cut down on the day of the battle. His fine head of hair, of which he was proud, betrays him; Absalom becomes entangled in the branches of a tree, and he is an easy target for David's men. At first, the soldiers are reluctant to strike, remembering the command of the king. Joab, David's general, strikes the key blow and brings death to the rebel. Absalom receives what he deserves, a just execution for his rebellion against his father and his attempt to seize the throne for himself.

Of course, the news must be sent to the king. Ordinarily, this news of victory on the battlefield would be good news to a king, but Joab knows how David will receive the report about the death of his son. Two messengers carry the news, one willingly carrying good news of victory without the sorrowful news of Absalom's death, and the second arriving with the very words that King David does not wish to hear.

David grieves deeply and sincerely over the death of his son. His grief is so overwhelming that at first he cannot hide it from his troops. Joab is forced to rebuke his king and to remind David of his responsibility to the army and to the nation. David must at least pretend to be glad that he won the war instead of losing to Absalom. David must welcome the troops home and congratulate them on their victory. With a heavy heart, David does what is required of him. The nation is still his, and he will still rule over it, and his soldiers deserve his thanks for a job well done, even if he wishes that they had not done their job quite so well.

It is clear for us to see that David truly loved Absalom in spite of Absalom's sinful ways. It is also evident that Absalom's crimes were not sudden acts of passion; each of them was carefully plotted and planned and acted out after years of preparation. David must face the grief of a parent whose child has turned to wicked ways. When a dreadful crime is committed, even today, we often hear of the parents of the perpetrator grieving over the actions of their son or their daughter. They have done their best to raise the child in the right way, and they cannot imagine how a child they loved so much can be so evil and can do such terrible things.

God Himself knows this kind of grief all too well. He loves all the people He made, and He is both angered and saddened by the sins we commit. God is angry to see us hurt ourselves and one another and the beautiful world He made. God is angry to see us build barriers between ourselves and Him, knowingly breaking His rules, doing what He told us not to do, and failing to do what He made us to do and commanded us to do. As David cried over Absalom, so God grieves over us, hating the sins we commit even while still wanting to claim us as His children.

David lost a son to that son's wickedness, but the son of David had to die so David could keep his kingdom. God the Father also lost a Son because of wickedness, and the death of His Son allowed God to reclaim a kingdom. The huge difference is, of course, that Absalom was guilty and deserved to die, but Jesus was innocent and did not deserve to die. The wickedness that killed Jesus was our sins, not His sins, for He never committed any sins. Jesus did not rebel against His Father, but our rebellion was put on His shoulders, and so He died for us and, in the process, brought us back into the kingdom and the family of His Father.

6 Three Sons of David

In considering the conflict between Absalom and his father, David, perhaps we should also consider two other sons of David: the infant son of David and Bathsheba, who died as a baby, and Jesus, the eternal Son of David. We can see the biblical testimony of all three of these sons of David as corresponding with one another. The testimony of the two Old Testament sons of David inform us of and depict for us aspects of the life and work of Jesus, the eternal Son of David.

If the memory of that infant son of David and Bathsheba stands as a reminder to us of Jesus, bearing the guilt of his parents who were forgiven for their sin, how much more is Absalom, the adult son of David and Maacah, a reminder of Jesus. Does that seem like a shocking comparison? Perhaps so; but let's consider it nonetheless. We know that both Absalom the son of David and Jesus the Son of David died because of sin and rebellion. Both sons of David died while hanging from a tree. In both cases, the death of the son brought grief to the father, who still welcomed back the very people who had caused the death of the son.

Our sins killed Jesus; there is no other way to put it. He died because we have rebelled against God and have broken His commandments. Yet, in death, Jesus set us free from sin and guilt. In death, Jesus ensured that we will never receive the punishment we deserve. God the Father welcomes us into His kingdom and calls us His children because Jesus died to take away our sins. The grief of the Father at the death of His Son must still change to the joy of the Father at the rescue of His chosen people.

The other key difference is, of course, that Jesus did not remain dead and buried. The soldiers of Israel heaped stones upon the grave of Absalom, but the stone that sealed the grave of Jesus was removed by angels to show that the grave was empty and that Jesus had risen from the dead. He died to bring us into His kingdom, but He lives to rule that kingdom. His Father's grief at the wickedness of the cross is now joy at the victory over sin and evil and death. We share that joy because, through Jesus, we also are victors over sin and evil and death.

Conclusion

There is such a stark contrast for us between Absalom and Jesus. Absalom, in his arrogance, thought that he could claim a kingdom that did not belong to him. Jesus, in humble obedience, has received a kingdom that has always belonged to Him. The one who was sinful and rebellious was the one who tried to seize the kingdom. The kingdom, to Absalom, was everything. And we know that, for us, the kingdom is everything as well.

Entrance into the kingdom of God means everything to us. We know that as sinners, we do not deserve a place in God's kingdom, and nothing we do can claim for us a place there. But as we saw with Absalom, there is always the temptation to assume that we deserve a place in that kingdom and can simply take it or claim it or earn it for ourselves. But as Absalom's attempt to take the kingdom of his father by his own efforts eventually failed, we know also that those who think that they deserve a place in the kingdom of heaven and try to claim it for themselves will also fail. In the end, they will be rejected. On the other hand, those who humbly confess their sins and seek salvation from their Savior are guaranteed a home in heaven. What we cannot take for ourselves is given to us at no cost to us. Jesus, the Son of David and the Son of God, has already done everything necessary to make us God's children forever.

Concluding Activities

Speak a closing prayer, make any necessary announcements, and distribute study leaflet 9.

Number the People

2 Samuel 20–24

Preparing for the Session

Central Focus

By grace, God converts the sinful census of Israel and its consequences into an opportunity for His love and mercy to prevail at the site of the temple.

Objectives

That participants, led by the Holy Spirit working through God's Word, will

1. perceive the subtle distinction between temptation and testing;

2. recognize the sin of pride in David's arbitrary census; and

3. see how grace triumphs over judgment in David's life and in their lives.

Note for the small-group leaders: Lesson notes and other materials you will need begin on page 67.

For the Lecture Leader

Session Plan

Worship

Begin the session with the hymn printed in the study leaflet. Accompaniments are available in denominational hymnals, such as *Lutheran Service Book* or *Lutheran Worship*. (Note: Concordia Publishing House has available *The Concordia Organist*. All the initial worship hymns in the LifeLight courses are included in this resource. It's especially helpful for mission congregations and small parishes. See the list of study resources on page 7.) Follow with this prayer:

Prayer

Holy and gracious God, You allow us to be tested by temptations and to feel, at times, the consequences of our sins, yet You sent Your Son to pay the full price for all our sins and to restore us into Your family. Grant that when we see our sins, we will not lose hope but will confess our sins and find comfort and hope in the victory won over sin and death by Your Son, Jesus Christ, for He lives and reigns with You and the Holy Spirit, one God, now and forever. Amen.

Lecture Presentation

1 Introduction

Every ten years, the United States government conducts a census, counting all the people who live in the country. Most other modern nations also conduct such numberings, although the schedule is different in different lands. Such counting, in the United States, is required by the Constitution to determine representation in Congress. The numbers gathered have hundreds of uses beyond that simple purpose. Funding of schools and roads and hundreds of other government projects is shaped by the census. Family researchers and historians use old census records to learn about people. The census can be important and valuable to a lot of people for many different reasons.

Such counting of people has been happening for a long, long time. We even see several instances of it in the Bible. For instance, Moses counted the Israelites at Mount Sinai after they had left Egypt, and he counted them again after their forty years of wandering in the wilderness. The Book of Numbers even derives its name from these two censuses of Israel. In the New Testament, we find that when Caesar Augustus issued a decree that all the people under Roman authority should be counted and taxed, Joseph took his bride, Mary, from Nazareth to Bethlehem so that they and the Son of Mary would be counted in the city of Bethlehem as sons and heirs of King David.

During the United States census of 2010, a small number of Americans grumbled about the census and suggested that it was asking too many questions and requiring too much information from American citizens. No one, though, insisted that conducting a census was sinful, or even illegal. The census that David conducted, however, appears to have been sinful and evil and should not even have been performed.

Over the centuries, God's people have struggled to determine what was wrong with the idea of counting the people of Israel at that time. Jewish historian and famous author Josephus lived at the time when Jerusalem was destroyed, forty years after the death and resurrection of Jesus. Josephus thought that David's sin was not that he had people counted, but that David forgot to collect a tax with the counting for the honor of God, as Moses had done. A more common explanation is that, by counting the people he ruled, David was expressing sinful pride, focusing more on himself than on God's blessings. In either case, the Bible is clear that David did sin by this action and that he did bring God's judgment upon himself.

2 God Does Not Tempt (2 Samuel 24:1–9)

The census that Moses conducted was not sinful. The census that Moses conducted obeyed a command of God. What is troubling about the description of David's decision to count the Israelites is that this also seems to follow a suggestion of God. In 2 Samuel 24:1 we read, "Again the anger of the LORD was kindled against Israel, and He incited David against them, saying, 'Go, number Israel and Judah.'" This verse raises some important questions about the God of the Bible. Does He tempt people to sin so He can punish them? Does God have the kind of personality that becomes bored when things are going well and so seeks to stir up trouble? If God is like this, He does not deserve our faith and our worship.

To help clarify this matter, we can recall that God is holy. That means that, among other things, He does not cause sins to happen. Not only does He not bring sins about, but He also does not ever want anyone to sin. However, we also know that God is all-knowing; He can foresee sin. And we know that God does not let His foreknowledge go to waste, but puts it to good use—and even for our benefit.

Scripture repeatedly shows us that God can allow sin to happen and then use it to accomplish greater good, as when He foresaw and used the plan of Judas to betray Jesus. God allowed the brothers of Joseph, son of Jacob, to sell him into slavery, beginning a series of events that gave Joseph control of Egypt during a famine and also the power to save the lives of his family. Even if God foresees sin and uses it in His plan, though, we cannot say that God approves of sin or that He tempts anyone to sin.

At times, though, it may be tempting for us to think that way. Perhaps there have been times when it seemed as though the deck was stacked against us and we had no acceptable option but to follow a course we knew Scripture condemned. Do we justify our actions to ourselves by thinking along these lines: "Clearly God wanted it this way or He would have given me more options"? Or perhaps at times, when suffering from the natural consequences of our transgressions, we bitterly blame God for giving us no other options. In other words, we essentially think that our sinning was all His fault because He did not provide us with a path to follow that was both easy and holy. Do we convince ourselves that God is to blame rather than ourselves?

But is that ever truly the case? James wrote, (1:13–14) "Let no one say when he is tempted, 'I am being tempted by God,' for God cannot be tempted with evil, and He Himself tempts no one. But each person is tempted when he is lured and enticed by his own desire." For this reason, in 1 Chronicles it is written, (21:1) "Then Satan stood against Israel and incited David to number Israel." Temptations do not come from God: they come from the devil and from the sinful world around us and from the sinful nature inside each of us. Yet, God is the Creator of all things and remains in control of all things. He could protect us from any temptation that we might not be able to resist. (He probably does this far more often than we realize or imagine.) When evil happens, God has allowed it to happen, and He has done so in great wisdom and great love, permitting that evil as part of His greater plan for good. Clearly, as is seen from 1 Chronicles, that was the case with the census of David, and just as clearly, it is the case for us as well.

3 God Does Test (2 Samuel 24:1–9)

God does not tempt anyone to sin, but God does test His people. This much Scripture makes very clear. For example, in Genesis 22, we read that God tested Abraham by commanding him to sacrifice his son Isaac on Mount Moriah. Abraham traveled for three days to that mountain with his son and was prepared on the third day to kill him, but God intervened and Abraham received his son back alive. Abraham was strengthened by this experience (and Isaac was strengthened as well, no doubt). Not only did Abraham see that his faith was strong enough to accomplish whatever God asked, but he also performed a dramatic demonstration of the sacrifice God would one day offer, giving His own Son as a sacrifice to redeem the world.

Does God doing this to Abraham and Isaac seem cruel to us? Does it seem like something sinister? Not only this example but also the very notion of God testing His people may strike us as being wrong. After all, people generally think of tests as tricks and traps designed to cause mistakes. A real test is meant to strengthen and improve, not to weaken and ensnare. The language of testing comes from metalworking, when metal is "tested" in fire to make it stronger. St. Peter, as an example, uses this analogy: (1 Peter 1:6–7) "In this you rejoice, though now for a little while, if necessary, you have been grieved by various trials, so that the tested genuineness of your faith—more precious than gold that perishes though it is tested by fire—may be found to result in praise and glory and honor at the revelation of Jesus Christ." The idea is that the trial they had been facing tested them, just as fire tested (and therefore improved) gold.

Of course, when most of us think of testing, we think of tests we took in school. A good test in school is not intended to cause students to make mistakes; a good test gives students a chance to show what they have learned. Although, to the students, tests may seem like a painful form of harassment, that really is not the case. A skillful teacher can use a test to teach, reinforcing the knowledge and skills that students have already gained. In the end, the students are better off for having prepared for and taken the test. In the same way, when God tests His people, even by allowing temptations or other forms of evil, His intention is not to trick and trap them, but to strengthen their faith and to give them opportunities to live according to that faith. Though at times our testing may be painful, God is never harassing us or causing us harm, but is helping and strengthening us.

God does not need to test us to learn about us, because God already knows everything about us. God provides tests to strengthen us, even when He knows that we will fail some of His tests. We can keep that in mind when we consider the early chapters of Genesis. In the Garden of Eden, God gave Adam and Eve several commands: they were to be fruitful and multiply and fill the earth, they were to take care of the Garden, and they were to refrain from eating fruit from a certain tree. We remember the command they failed to obey, and some people accuse God of being unfair, giving them that opportunity to sin. However, we should also remember that, had they obeyed His command, they would have had a joyful experience of doing what was right to please God. Surely such an experience would have been of tremendous benefit to them. And most likely, after the times of testing, that tree would have had a different purpose in their future lives, but we do not know that purpose. We only know what did happen. Adam and Eve did what they chose rather than what God commanded, and we have been living with the consequences of their wrong choice ever since.

The wages of sin is death. That is stated for us very clearly in Romans 6:23. We also see it depicted for us vividly in Genesis 3, in the account of the fall into sin in the Garden of Eden. When Adam and Eve sinned, they died, even though their bodies lived on for hundreds of years. Their sin placed barriers between themselves and God. Their sin placed barriers between the two of them. Their sin placed barriers between them and the good world God had made. Their sin placed barriers even between the people they had been created to be and the people they now were. Each of these barriers was a little death, pointing forward to the death of the body and eternal death separated from God. The tempter had told them that choosing for themselves rather than obeying would make them like God, but sinning made Adam and Eve less like God than before. They had been perfect in love for God and love for each other; now they were selfish, putting themselves before God and each other. They had been connected by love to all that surrounded them, but those barriers crushed the connections that love had established and cut them off from the source of life.

When God spoke to Adam and Eve about their sin, He did not only judge and condemn them; He also gave them the hope of the Gospel. He promised that a descendant would come from their family who would crush the devil's head. He promised new life, even as their sin removed them from their old life. God instituted the promise of a sacrifice as He sent the people He loved from the garden to the wilderness. This sacrifice would be pictured again and again through history as God's people waited for the sacrifice of God's own Son, the sacrifice that would crush evil and restore the world to God's perfect plan.

4 The Hands of the Lord (2 Samuel 24:10–25)

God spoke these Gospel promises because He is a God of love and of mercy and of grace. We see this same grace and mercy at work even after David sinned by ordering the census. When David sinned, and when God allowed him a choice of consequences to follow that sin, David chose wisely: (2 Samuel 24:14) "Let us fall into the hand of the Lord, for His mercy is great." Three days of pestilence struck Israel as a result of David's choice, but at the end of those three days, when David saw God's angel about to strike Jerusalem, he called for mercy and his prayer was heard.

"Let us fall into the hand of the LORD." This saying of David is one that could equally be the prayer of us all. "Let us fall into the hand of the LORD," for with Him there truly is mercy and forgiveness. All of the books of the Bible proclaim this to us. His grace toward us knows no measure, and His love for us is infinite.

In acknowledgement of God's act of mercy, David then purchased the place where he had seen the angel of the Lord withdraw his sword of judgment. He bought the threshing floor of Araunah the Jebusite, and there he built an altar and sacrificed to the Lord. This threshing floor was located on one of the hills of Jerusalem, a hill called Moriah. On this same hill (perhaps at or nearby the very same spot!), Abraham had prepared to offer his son Isaac and had received him back alive a thousand years before the time of David. On this same hill, on the land David purchased, Solomon his son would build the temple of the Lord. The sacrifices God had commanded through Moses had been offered up until that time at the tabernacle, a tent that moved with the Israelites as they traveled from place to place. When the temple was built by Solomon, it was the only place where sacrifices could be offered to God.

On a skull-shaped outcropping of that same hill (or if not that hill, then one nearby) a thousand years after the time of David, the Son of David would be offered as the ultimate sacrifice, that sacrifice of which all other sacrifices were only pictures. As Solomon's temple was the only place where sacrifices could be offered to God, so is Jesus the only sacrifice acceptable to God. His sacrifice is the only way to remove the guilt of sin and to restore God's favor and blessing to sinners. The Gospel of God continues unchanged, from the promise to Adam and Eve, to the promise to Abraham, to the promise to David, to the promise fulfilled in Christ. That same unchanging promise continues to be shared with the world today, the good news that Jesus has paid for all sins, and that in Him is found the mercy and grace of God.

God had told Abraham that his descendants would be uncountable, like the stars in the sky or the sand on the ground. David, in his pride, attempted to put a number to the citizens of Israel, but even that number was meaningless. Through Christ, many more have entered the family of Abraham, for the Christian Church in every land and in every century has been adding to the number of those who share the faith of Abraham and belong to his family. All those who trust in the promise of God are saved by the fulfillment of that promise in Christ. A census brought judgment on David and on God's people, but another census brought Mary and Joseph to Bethlehem so that the Son of David could be born in that city and could begin His path to the cross.

Conclusion

The motto of the Lutheran Reformation is frequently repeated: faith alone, grace alone, Scripture alone. Behind all three of these is a fourth: Christ alone. Faith is not saving faith if it is not faith in Christ. Grace is not true grace if it is not God's grace delivered through Christ. Scripture is not a message of salvation unless Christ is sought in it. Clearly, from our study of the Books of 1 and 2 Samuel, we should be able, all the more confidently, to confess Christ alone. For here in these Old Testament books we have clearly seen God working His grace among His people—a grace that was based upon the incarnation of the One who had not yet come. From the prayer of Hannah to the altar of David, the Books of 1 and 2 Samuel teach about the mission of Jesus Christ, the Son of God and the Son of David.

Some of those lessons are clear prophecies of Christ, such as Nathan's assurance that God would build David a house and David's Son would rule an eternal kingdom. Some of these lessons are pictures that remind Christians of Jesus, such as the sons of David who died: one who suffered because of the guilt of his father, and another who died hanging on a tree. Whenever we read the Bible, we search the Scriptures, looking for Christ. The more we expect to find Him, the more we learn about Jesus, even from the history of His people a thousand years before He was born.

Concluding Activities

Speak an appropriate closing prayer and announce the next LifeLight topic.

Small-Group Leaders Material

Samuel anoints David, fresco, ca. 239 AD / © Art Resource, NY

The Word of the Lord Was Rare

1 Samuel 1–6

Preparing for the Session

Central Focus

In Samuel's time, and in our time as well, knowledge of God's Word may be lacking, even among those who are surrounded by God's gifts of grace.

Objectives

That participants, led by the Holy Spirit working through God's Word, will

1. remember and rejoice in the power of God's Means of Grace—His Word and His Sacraments;
2. realize that faith is not guaranteed by mere exposure to the Means of Grace; and
3. resolve to be active in the use of the Means of Grace through regular Bible reading and active membership in a faithful congregation.

For the Small-Group Leader

Small-Group Discussion Helps

Day 1 • 1 Samuel 1

1. Hannah's husband has another wife who has borne children, but Hannah is not a mother. Children in Israel were valuable both to inherit family property and to care for their parents in their later years. For these reasons, Hannah prays to the Lord for a son.

2. Eli assumes that Hannah is drunk and scolds her for the sin he thinks she has committed. Since the priest represents God in Old Testament Israel, his words can be considered judgment from the Lord.

3. First, Eli understands Hannah's situation and blesses her instead of judging her. Second, Hannah does conceive and bear a son.

4. As she vowed, Hannah has her son Samuel live at the tabernacle as a servant to the Lord and to his priests.

5. Participants may share a number of helpful words of advice and comfort. Among them might be the assurance that God does hear all prayers and does provide His people with what He knows is best, and that God works on His own schedule, which does not always match our schedules. God can be trusted to care for His people, even when He does not grant us what we think is right for us. Additional loving and faithful expressions of advice and comfort should be encouraged.

Day 2 • 1 Samuel 2

6. While much of what Hannah says is general, her words about "the barren" in verse 5 apply to her situation. Her reference to "arrogance" (v. 3) may reflect her relationship with Peninnah, her husband's other wife (see 1:6). Almost the entire song, though, could be sung by any believer.

7. The Book of Luke begins with similar songs. There also, a woman (Elizabeth) bears a child after being barren for many years; this child (John the Baptist), like Samuel, will be a special servant to the Lord.

8. Eli's sons were interfering with the offerings of the Israelites, taking what they wanted rather than what the Law of the Lord assigned to them. As priests of the Lord, they were expected to honor and respect God's Word and to teach it to others, rather than causing people to resent the priesthood and the worship of the Lord. Then as now, when people who claim to work for the Lord only seek their own wealth or comfort or power, they cause others to doubt the goodness of God and drive them away from the Lord. This is a serious sin that grieves the Lord and causes His wrath.

9. A "man of God" (a prophet) speaks words of warning and judgment (vv. 27–36). These words will be repeated by God in chapter 3, spoken directly to Samuel.

10. God promises a faithful priest who will do the work that a priest should do; He also promises that this priest will provide help even to those who have sinned and brought judgment against themselves. This promise was first fulfilled in the career of Samuel, but its greater fulfillment is in the work of Jesus Christ, the Great High Priest (see Hebrews 4:14–16).

Day 3 • 1 Samuel 3

11. God stands in the Most Holy Place and calls Samuel by name. He gives him a message of judgment against Eli and his family. What a sign of grace that God would come to Samuel and chose him to speak for the Lord.

12. God threatens punishment and destruction and says that no sacrifice or offering will be sufficient to remove this judgment. Eli accepts this message with the words "It is the Lord. Let Him do what seems good to Him" (v. 18).

13. "Samuel grew, and the Lord was with him and let none of his words fall to the ground" (v. 19). Compare Luke 2:52: "And Jesus increased in wisdom and in stature and in favor with God and man."

14. Clearly, we can see that the similarities noted above are not coincidental. Luke, guided by the Holy Spirit, deliberately uses similar language to show how Samuel was a picture of Jesus, the Great High Priest who will reconcile sinners to God (note answer 10, above).

Day 4 • 1 Samuel 4–5

15. The Israelites are reminding themselves and God of God's promise to be with them and to give them victory over their enemies. The Philistines are also aware of this promise; the presence of the ark frightens them.

16. The ark is captured by the Philistines. This shows that God has turned His back on His people, who first turned their backs on Him by following other gods and by allowing the priesthood to become corrupt. As a result of God's rejection, the Israelites lose the battle, and the sons of Eli are killed. Also, Eli the high priest dies when he learns what has happened, all fulfilling the twice-delivered warning from the Lord.

17. The statue of the Philistine god Dagon topples before the ark of the covenant; on the second occasion, the statue is broken. This shows the Philistines that their god is weak. It shows that the Lord of Israel is the only true God.

18. People become sick and die. (The mention of rats and tumors suggests bubonic plague.) This demonstrates that, while God is merciful to those who come to Him in faith, His presence means judgment and destruction to those who come to Him without faith.

19. The Philistines react with fear and want every reminder of God's presence to go far away. People today who do not believe God's promises still react to reminders of God with fear, wanting to make these reminders go far away.

Day 5 • 1 Samuel 6

20. The Philistines decide to return the ark to Israel, but they choose to do so in a way that proves that God is in control.

21. Evidently, the Philistines are uncertain whether the things that have been happening are from God or are mere coincidences. The unnatural behavior of the cows, leaving behind their young, is one more indication that God's presence is with the ark of the covenant and that He is in control of all things.

22. Their first reaction is joy, and they offer a thank-offering to the Lord.

23. Some of the Israelites try to look inside the ark. God had forbidden people to touch the ark, and so they are killed. God wants His Word to be taken seriously by His people. His commands and His warnings of judgment are to be taken seriously, as are also His promises of grace and mercy.

24. They call to a group of priests to take care of the ark. Only the priests were allowed to deal with the ark (and they were instructed to carry it on poles, not to touch it directly). All of this reminds the Israelites of that time, and Bible readers today, that holy things are to be taken seriously, not to be treated lightly.

Appoint for Us a King

1 Samuel 7–12

Preparing for the Session

Central Focus

Our attitude toward the authority of human government reflects and reveals our attitude toward the Lord of lords.

Objectives

That participants, led by the Holy Spirit working through God's Word, will

1. understand the reasons why Samuel did not want to anoint a king over Israel;
2. understand the reasons why God chose to place a king over Israel; and
3. see the relationship in their lives between human authority and God's authority.

For the Small-Group Leader

Small-Group Discussion Helps

Day 1 • 1 Samuel 7

1. Put away the foreign gods and trust only in the Lord (v. 3).

2. The Lord thundered and threw the Philistines into a panic (v. 10), and the Israelites defeated them (v. 11).

3. We cannot buy God's favor with our words or with our obedience. Although we should still say and do the right things, that does not cause God to love us. God loves us because love is His nature and because Christ has died to redeem us and to bring us back to God, erasing all our sins. At times, God does permit His people to suffer, even when they say and do the right things. At times, God does permit the wicked to prosper. We say and do the right things even in those times, trusting that God still loves us and that He will rescue us according to His promises and on His own schedule.

4. The stone is a monument, set up to remind the people how God had helped them. Earlier patriarchs had also set up stones as reminders, just as people use crosses today as reminders of what Christ has done. The reminders have no special power beyond their purpose to help us remember what God has done.

5. He "judged Israel all the days of his life" (v. 15), traveling around the land to teach the Israelites and remind them of God's commands and His promises.

Day 2 • 1 Samuel 8

6. Samuel's sons "turned aside after gain" and "took bribes and perverted justice" (v. 3). In this, they were much like the sons of Eli.

7. The Israelites asked Samuel to choose a king for them. They did not want to be ruled by Samuel's sons, and they wanted to have the same kind of government as other nations, rather than trusting that God would raise up faithful judges like Samuel.

8. Samuel was displeased and warned the people of all the problems they would have if they were ruled by a king. He convinced them that their desire for a king was sinful. God, on the other hand, said that Samuel should do as they asked, reminding Samuel that the people were rejecting God and not Samuel.

9. Samuel warned that the king would take some of everything that belonged to the people—their children, their land, their money, and their workers. He threatened a 10 percent tax required by the kings (making the kings equal to God, who also demanded 10 percent of their income be given to Him). He said that, when the people trusted their king and were disappointed, then God would not answer their prayers, because they had chosen a king instead of Him.

10. Most governments require all these things from their citizens; in fact, a 10 percent tax would be considered surprisingly low in many situations today. Although people honor God by obeying their government, when forced to choose, Christians "must obey God rather than men" (Acts 5:29). A Christian's loyalty to nation and to government remains "under God" and not instead of God.

Day 3 • 1 Samuel 9–10

11. Saul is a handsome young man from a wealthy family, taller than most other men. He is not seeking to rule a kingdom, but only to take care of his family's property. His tribe and his clan are the humblest in the land, not the family where one would expect to find a king.

12. Saul treats Samuel, the man of God, as a seer and not as the Lord's messenger. He tends to treat the work of Samuel as that of a magician who can find missing items and tell him the future. This shows how many other people in Israel viewed their relationship with the Lord and with His Word.

13. Samuel works within Saul's understanding of religion to prepare him to be king of Israel. Saul is overpowered by the Holy Spirit to show that the Spirit of God will be with him as king, but also to humble him and remind him that he still serves under God rather than in the place of God.

14. Samuel draws lots to choose the tribe, the clan, and the family of the king. This shows that God is in control and that Samuel is not choosing by wealth or power or reputation. Saul hides, possibly because he has become frightened by the responsibility that has been given to him, or possibly also to show that he is not seeking the power over the kingdom that is being given to him.

15. Some honor Saul, but others speak against him. This shows that, like other times in the history of Israel, the nation was not united. Almost always among sinners, some will accept what happens while others complain; some will seek to honor and serve God while others rebel against His will.

Day 4 • 1 Samuel 11

16. An attack by Ammon, followed by insults when diplomacy is attempted, provokes Saul to raise and lead an army.

17. Saul was plowing a field, still caring for his family land. Israel did not need a full-time king as yet, but could have a part-time king who also had time to work on the farm. Also, they probably had not gathered enough wealth to support a king and a royal court.

18. Saul is completely successful in his battle against the Ammonites. Of course, God deserves full credit for the success of Saul and of Israel's army.

19. The country gathers behind the king, to the point that many citizens want to punish those who earlier spoke against the king. Saul does not want to punish anyone on this day of his victory, because he wants all people to celebrate what God has done. Saul's words, "today the Lord has worked salvation in Israel" (v. 13), signify that he sees that his success is due to the Lord's work. They also show that those who sinned against him in the past are forgiven due to the work God has done in Israel.

20. Participants may note the importance of supporting the government rather than complaining against it, although others may defend the importance of freedom of speech and the ability citizens have in the modern world to vote to replace their leaders with new leaders. Participants may also comment on the austerity of Saul's rule, that he did not make great demands on the nation as Samuel had threatened. Finally, participants are likely to comment on the importance of recognizing God's lordship over the nation at all times, especially at times of need. Other thoughts may also be offered.

Day 5 • 1 Samuel 12

21. Samuel says that he has stolen nothing, defrauded no one, accepted no bribes, and not misused his authority in any other way. The people agree that he has been honest in his leadership.

22. Samuel reminds the people that God has always cared for them, even when they fell short of His commands. He calls on the people to continue to trust God and be faithful to Him.

23. The Israelites repent of their sins and ask for forgiveness.

24. Samuel promises to continue to pray for the people, and he promises that God will not forsake them. (This chapter could be compared to the farewell sermon of Joshua near the end of that book.)

25. Christians today should also resolve to put God first and to honor Him and obey His commands. Also, like Samuel, Christians should pray for their leaders and for their fellow citizens, seeking God's guidance and protection for all the people of the nation.

In the Name of the LORD of Hosts

1 Samuel 13–18

Preparing for the Session

Central Focus

David prevailed over Goliath, not because he believed in himself or in his cause, but because he trusted God's promises.

Objectives

That participants, led by the Holy Spirit working through God's Word, will

1. comprehend the politics and military strategy involving the Israelites and Philistines three thousand years ago;
2. recognize David's faith in God's promises as his source of strength, confidence, and victory; and
3. apply the same confidence in the Lord to their personal battles with evil, sin, and temptation, recognizing Christ's victory in all these struggles.

For the Small-Group Leader

Small-Group Discussion Helps

Day 1 • 1 Samuel 13

1. Some participants may state that their confidence in the Bible is decreased by this omission. If the original numbers written by the author of the book have been lost, participants may then wonder how many other portions of the Bible have been lost or changed over time. Others may indicate that the loss of these numbers indicates God's judgment on Saul, that even his age and the length of his reign have been cut short by the Holy Spirit in God's Word. In either case, all participants should remember that the Bible is trustworthy and true in all matters relating to faith. Although doubts exist about certain numbers or about the accurate translation of certain words (especially rare animals, plants, or gems), the actual message of the Bible is not altered in any way.

2. The Philistines are far stronger and more numerous than the Israelites. Many Israelites either hide or flee. 3. Saul's sacrifice is a major mistake, not only because he did something he had not been told to do, but also because he did the job of a priest, even though he came from the tribe of Benjamin and not from the tribe of Levi. Only the Messiah could combine the jobs of king and priest, and Saul was not the Messiah. Saul therefore attacks the promise of the Messiah by taking on His role without the Lord's permission or direction.

4. Iron is a stronger metal than bronze, so it would be more effective as a weapon, and also as a tool for farming. Iron Age cultures could be expected to defeat Bronze Age cultures on the battlefield and to outperform them in peaceful arenas as well.

5. Israel, however, has the blessing of the Lord and His promises; this makes them stronger than the Philistines (but only when they remember this advantage and trust His promises).

Day 2 • 1 Samuel 14

6. Jonathan and his armor-bearer go among the Philistines, killing about twenty of them and throwing them into a panic. Jonathan knows the power and the promises of God, saying, "nothing can hinder the LORD from saving by many or by few" (v. 6).

7. Saul imposes a fast upon himself and the entire army of Israel, promising that no one will eat until evening. This weakens the soldiers, making them less able to defeat the Philistines. Their hunger also causes them to eat the blood with the meat when they slaughter animals after sundown, thus sinning against the commands of God. Finally, Saul's curse falls upon Jonathan, who did not know about his father's vow, and Jonathan nearly is killed by the command of his father.

8. Thanks to the courage of Jonathan, the Israelites do prevail against the Philistines, in spite of their weakness due to hunger. Saul reminds the people of God's commands and provides a way for them to prepare their meat in a way that is clean. The army speaks on behalf of Jonathan and refuses to allow Saul to keep his word and kill the man who violated the king's vow.

9. God's name is holy and should be treated as holy. The Second Commandment warns us not to misuse God's name, and in the Lord's Prayer we are taught to

pray, "Hallowed be Thy name." When a promise or vow is made in the name of the Lord, God holds us to our words by the power of His name, even if our promise or vow is foolish. Therefore, Jesus encourages us not to use God's name lightly: "Let what you say be simply 'Yes' or 'No'; anything more than this comes from evil" (Matthew 5:37).

10. Participants may think of many examples of foolish promises, especially those spoken in times of danger or worry. Often, people decide not to carry through on these promises, thus increasing the barrier between themselves and God. All sins are forgiven by Christ because of His sacrifice on the cross, even sins of foolish promises, whether they are kept or broken. All the same, God's name is holy and should never be used lightly.

Day 3 • 1 Samuel 15–16

11. Saul fails to destroy completely the Amalekites as God had commanded. Instead, he tries to keep the best for himself and his soldiers, then lies and says that he was going to give the best to God. Both the initial disobedience and the lie increase his separation from God, bringing further judgment upon himself. Saul is abusing his authority as king by leading the nation away from God instead of leading them according to God's Word.

12. The Bible teaches that the opportunity for repentance comes to an end and God no longer hears the prayers of sinners, even if they say the right words. See Romans 9:14–18 and Hebrews 10:26–31. These verses do not say that God created some people with the plan to judge and condemn them. They say simply that God withdraws the opportunity for repentance and renewal from those who have resolved to be His enemies. Because we do not know the mind of God, we continue to proclaim His Word to all sinners, calling for repentance and faith. We do so, knowing that some will reject the message. (Compare Mark 4:1–20.)

13. Samuel must protect himself and the king he anoints from Saul's animosity. Samuel does not lie, but he is less than fully honest. Such deception is not intended as a guide for God's people in most situations. When Christians must choose between conflicting commandments, though (such as telling a lie to preserve a life), they must do what they can to honor God and help their neighbors while also repenting of whatever sins they do commit, rejoicing to know that they are forgiven and saved through Christ's work and not by their own good works.

14. God tells Samuel whom to anoint, reminding him to follow God's guidance and not to trust his own perception. We learn that we do not need to be special in the eyes of other people to be chosen by God; God always chooses His people by grace and not by worldly standards.

15. David is brought to Saul as a musician to sing for Saul and calm him. Saul probably paid little attention to David's appearance when he sang. Because he was accustomed to see him and hear him only in the calmness of his court, he did not recognize David by appearance or by voice on the battlefield.

Day 4 • 1 Samuel 17

16. Both armies are camped on a hillside, and neither wants to begin the attack because the one that moves first will lose the advantage of the terrain. Goliath proposes single combat—himself against one Israelite fighter. Until David arrives, no one accepts Goliath's challenge because he is bigger and stronger and seems more likely to win such a combat.

17. David knows that Goliath has insulted Israel and God, so he expects God to defend Himself and His chosen people against Goliath. Also, David trusts that God will care for him because David has already been anointed to be the next king of Israel.

18. David refuses the armor and weapons of Saul because he is not used to them. However, he does prepare for combat using the tools with which he is familiar. David first stuns Goliath with a stone fired by a sling, then uses Goliath's own sword to cut off his head. The Philistines then flee, pursued by the Israelites.

19. The greatest enemies of every one of us are the devil, the sinful world around us, and the sin within each of us. Death is also the great enemy that faces every person. None of us can defeat these enemies with our own abilities and supplies.

20. Jesus is the warrior who has defeated the devil, the sinful world, the sins we have committed, and even death. David is a picture of Jesus as he battles Goliath and defeats him, trusting the promises of God and confident that God will overcome any enemy he faces.

Day 5 • 1 Samuel 18

21. Saul is frightened of David because David has become so popular in Israel. Saul already senses that David will replace him as king.

22. Saul first tries to kill David with a sudden throw of his spear, but David avoids that attack. Saul then puts David in a situation where David might be killed, challenging David to battle and kill more Philistines to earn the right to marry Saul's daughter.

23. Especially when David succeeds in killing Philistines, he becomes a greater hero and a greater threat to Saul's control of the kingdom.

24. Participants may think of many such instances, such as Joseph, the son of Jacob, who was sold as a slave and became de facto ruler of Egypt and a savior to his family.

25. God always wins because He is the Lord, in control of all events. He may allow His people to suffer for a time, but He has promised to take care of His people, and God always keeps His promises. The love and the promises of God should be stressed over the mere fact of His power and might.

David and His Merry Band of Outlaws
1 Samuel 19–24

Preparing for the Session

Central Focus

David, as an outsider, can be regarded as a picture of Christ and of His grace, prevailing over evil and also over the Law of God and its condemnation of sinners.

Objectives

That participants, led by the Holy Spirit working through God's Word, will

1. comprehend the relationship of Saul and David and observe its complexity;
2. see Jesus as the Savior who frees sinners from the condemnation of the Law; and
3. join with Jesus, not as rebels against God's Law, but as redeemed sinners, set free by the work of the Savior.

For the Small-Group Leader

Small-Group Discussion Helps

Day 1 • 1 Samuel 19

1. Jonathan and Michal are David's defenders in this chapter. The irony is that both Jonathan and Michal are children of King Saul; they work against their father to protect the man who will replace him.

2. Michal helps David to escape through a window. Then she assists his escape by putting an image (an idol from Canaanite religion) in David's bed so his enemies will think he is still in bed. Michal then defends herself by distorting the words David said to her to make it appear that he threatened her life.

3. In a perfect world, no one would sin or be tempted to sin. In a better world, perhaps no situation would arise in which people would have to choose between sinning in one way or another way, such as choosing between lying or contributing to a murder. In this sinful world, people must make such choices from time to time. Rather than defending the sin because of the circumstances, Christians rejoice to know that all their sins are forgiven, including those that they felt forced to commit in order to avoid greater sins.

4. At the beginning of his career, Saul was overwhelmed by the power of the Holy Spirit to remind him that God is in control and to humble Saul's view of himself. This second event reminds him and the people of Israel of the earlier occasion to make the same points: God is in control, and King Saul should be humble in the face of God's plans.

5. These reminders were written and preserved in the Bible to make the same points for people today, especially those in power. All people need to remember that God is in control, and all those with authority need to perform their duties with humility.

Day 2 • 1 Samuel 20

6. David and Jonathan would not normally be friends, because both of them know that David has been chosen by God to inherit the throne of Israel, but Jonathan would usually be expected to inherit the throne from his father, Saul. Moreover, Jonathan would normally support his father's will, and Saul wishes to destroy David.

7. In this account of their friendship, we see David and Jonathan both exhibit the qualities of loyalty and faithfulness to each other. They do not selfishly consider what would be best for them, but they each instead care about the other's needs.

8. David stays away from the royal table when he is expected to be there to provoke a reaction from Saul. This method of provoking Saul is safest for David, since he is far away from Saul when Saul becomes angry. It also reveals to Jonathan how unreasonable his father's anger with David truly is.

9. Jonathan pretends to be talking about arrows he has shot, when he is actually giving advice to David. This allows him to speak to David without any witnesses knowing that a message is being delivered. David's location is hidden from Saul, as is the fact that Jonathan is communicating with David. Therefore, their coded language provides safety to both men.

10. Participants may think of many examples. Perhaps some will remember the friendship between Jesus and

John, the disciple "whom He loved" (John 19:26). The fact that Jesus Himself had a best friend teaches us that God does approve of friendship. Though the greatest commandment is that we love God (Matthew 22:37–38), the second greatest is that we also are to love our neighbors (Matthew 22:39). This does not mean that we love them all equally; friendship is a genuine form of love, of which God approves.

Day 3 • 1 Samuel 21–22

11. One possible answer is that David's action was necessary to save lives, while Saul's was only a matter of convenience. Another is that David does not offer sacrifices as a priest (Saul's sin) but merely eats food generally reserved for the priests. See the next question for further consideration of this event.

12. Jesus uses this event to illustrate that God is not satisfied with slavish adherence to the Law (and especially adherence to human interpretations of God's Law) but that the Gospel prevails over the Law in the life of God's people. This lesson does not permit Christians to violate God's Law whenever they choose to do so. Instead, it reminds Christians that forgiveness covers all violations of the Law.

13. We are never "permitted" to break God's commands, but we are forgiven for all our sins. The important difference is not that we can justify the sin to ourselves, but that we know we are living under grace and not under Law. Therefore, when a sinful action appears necessary, we do the best we can, but we also continue living under forgiveness rather than proudly defending what we have done.

14. David pretended to be insane in Gath so he would be released from the king's power and sent away to a place where he could be safe. His strategy is successful. The fact that David once behaved in this manner is not license to imitate David's strategy. Neither does the Bible forbid and condemn such strategy. When Jesus told His apostles to be "wise as serpents and innocent as doves" (Matthew 10:16), He neither authorizes sin nor forbids His people to use their resources to protect themselves from danger.

15. Saul kills the priests and destroys the city as acts of war, indicating that he is at war with his own people over the issue of David as hero and future king. This complete destruction of a city of Levites puts Saul in a bad light, compared to the fact that he did not completely destroy the Amalekites when God commanded him to do so. Saul is continually moving farther away from God's will.

Day 4 • 1 Samuel 23

16. As an Israelite (and as the anointed king of Israel), David seeks to defend his own country from its enemies. Furthermore, his attack on the Philistines declares that David is not the enemy of Saul, even if Saul is the enemy of David. Finally, David has two clear messages from the Lord authorizing and commanding this attack.

17. Saul considers both David and the Philistines as enemies, and he attacks David because he fears David more than he fears the Philistines. A message from the Lord warns David of Saul's intentions and provides him the means of escape.

18. David firmly refuses to fight against his king, even when his king wants to fight him. David respects the office of king because Saul has been anointed to rule Israel and because the king rules the nation with authority that comes from God. Also, the king of Israel is a picture of the promised Messiah; David does not want to be seen fighting against this picture of the Messiah.

19. Christians obey the government except in cases where the government requires disobedience to God's commands. Christians honor their government, even when some positions and actions of that government are wrong.

20. When governments persecute their Christian citizens (as Saul persecuted David), Christians are permitted to flee. When Christian citizens have power (such as in fair elections) to change their government, they are right to do so; however, the Bible does not authorize violent resistance and rebellion.

Day 5 • 1 Samuel 24

21. David is hiding in a cave, and Saul uses the cave as a bathroom. David could kill Saul on this occasion, but he refuses.

22. Instead of killing Saul, David cuts off part of Saul's clothing to prove that he could have hurt Saul but refused. This is meant to show Saul that David does not consider himself Saul's enemy.

23. Saul speaks words of repentance and reconciliation with David. Although Saul admits that David is right and that he himself is wrong, he later goes back on these words.

24. God's Word commands us to be kind and merciful and not to seek revenge against those who hurt us (or try to hurt us). We are being like Christ when we forgive our enemies and pray for those who persecute us. In this Christlike behavior, we also bear witness to the truth and power of the Gospel, which forgives sins and also overcomes evil with good.

25. We seek to obey the commands of God, especially those that require us to forgive our enemies and to be kind to all people, even those that oppose us. When things go wrong for us because of sin in the world, we remember that Christ triumphed over sin and evil on the cross and that His victory belongs to us because of His grace. We remain patient and wait for the Day of the Lord, rather than trusting in our own power to triumph over evil (for, apart from Christ, we will lose such a battle).

Four Remarkable Women

1 Samuel 25–31

Preparing for the Session

Central Focus

God works through various kinds of people to accomplish His plan in the world.

Objectives

That participants, led by the Holy Spirit working through God's Word, will

1. acknowledge that women, as well as men, have a place in God's plan;

2. understand that the key difference between people is the presence or absence of faith in Christ and His promises; and

3. rejoice to know that even sinners can accomplish important roles in God's plan.

For the Small-Group Leader

Small-Group Discussion Helps

Day 1 • 1 Samuel 25

1. David asks that his men receive a share of the holiday meal at sheep-shearing time, since they have voluntarily protected the flocks and shepherds of Nabal from danger. Nabal refuses, because he claims not to know David or his men, and he says it would be wrong to share his wealth and the reward of his workers with strangers. (Nabal may also be considering the political consequences of supporting David while Saul is still the enemy of David, although the Bible does not mention this possibility.)

2. David is prepared to attack Nabal and destroy him and his property. He has been insulted by Nabal's refusal to share what he has with the men who have protected him, and David takes this refusal as a personal attack.

3. Abigail brings gifts to David and his men, doing what David had asked in the place of her husband. She agrees with David that her husband was wrong, but by doing what he refused to do, she prevents David's plan of revenge from taking place.

4. When David is prevented from completing his plan of revenge, God allows Nabal to be struck with illness, and Nabal dies. This judgment may be medically a direct result of Nabal's excessive celebration, since he has kept the good things for himself and has not shared them with his worthy neighbors. David marries Abigail, receiving the wealth of Nabal, which he would have destroyed in his act of revenge.

5. Participants' responses will vary, and many may not wish to answer aloud such a personal question. We can find comfort in the way that God protected David from temptation and from the sin of revenge when David was already giving in to temptation and preparing to act upon his anger. God continues to bless David, even when David sins and falls short of God's perfect plan; therefore, we know that God will forgive us and bless us, even when we fall short of His perfect plan.

Day 2 • 1 Samuel 26–27

6. David's reasons remain unchanged: he respects the office of the king because the king represents God's authority, because David knows he someday will hold this office, and because he respects the king as a picture of the promised Messiah ("the Lord's anointed").

7. As David has twice refused to lift his hand against Saul, so God has not yet brought judgment upon Saul. David knows that God's judgment will come—"the Lord will strike him, or his day will come to die, or he will go down into battle and perish" (26:10)—but David refuses to take matters into his own hands and kill Saul.

8. David now believes that he will be safer in Gath than in Israel; he also is confident that Saul will not pursue him into foreign territory.

9. David attacks enemies of Israel that live south of the border, but he tells the Philistines that he has been raiding the towns of Israel.

10. David considered this deception necessary because he thought that the Philistines would trust him only if he appeared to be attacking the Israelites.

Day 3 • 1 Samuel 28

11. Mediums claim to be able to deliver messages from the spiritual realms, especially messages from the spirits or ghosts of people who have died. God forbids His people from trying to communicate with the spirits of those who have died. He wants us to trust Him alone, to pray only to Him, and to seek guidance for the future from His Word. Those who seek messages from ghosts are, among other things, doubting what God says about His victory over death and about the resurrection to everlasting life.

12. God frequently uses ways of communicating with people other than those in which He has promised to be found. He does not want His people to use or to trust these other means (such as dreams or casting lots), but God is willing to use them when He wants to deliver a message to someone who is not seeking God in the means that God has chosen.

13. Christians have always known that sinners rebelling against God can still perform virtuous acts. Good deeds do not save people from their sins, and good deeds are not always caused by faith in God. We thank God for the good things that unbelievers do apart from His grace, even as we continue to share the Gospel of salvation with sinners—even virtuous sinners—so that they too can be saved from sin and evil through Christ.

14. God's commands and His judgment upon sinners can be known in a number of ways, but His grace and salvation are known only through the means God has chosen. As an unrepentant sinner, Saul is subject to God's judgment, and because he does not trust God's mercy, he does not receive God's Means of Grace. This fact does not prevent God from speaking Law and condemnation to Saul in a different way.

15. Christians should not seek to know God through other religions, even when those other religions appear to comprehend at least some of the demands of God's Law. Christians find reliable messages from God only in the Bible and in the Church gathered around the Bible and the Sacraments of Baptism and Communion.

Day 4 • 1 Samuel 29–30

16. The Philistines fear that on the battlefield David and his men will turn against them and join with Israel's army. David complains about the fact that the Philistines do not trust him.

17. Opinions will vary. Since David has been lying to the Philistines about his campaigns, it seems likely that he does plan to deceive them on the battlefield. God may have protected David from committing this act of treachery as he did from David's desire to take revenge against Nabal.

18. The home of David and his men is raided by the Amalekites, who carry away property and prisoners. If David and his men had remained with the Philistines, they would have arrived home too late to rescue their families and their possessions. Clearly, God is in control of events here, as always.

19. David finds an Egyptian abandoned by the Amalekites, receives information about where they are, pursues them, overtakes them, and destroys them, recapturing their prisoners and plunder. Some of his men are too tired to take part in the pursuit and battle, so they remain behind. David rewards them equally with those who fought, making holding a place in his army more significant than battlefield accomplishments.

20. Opinions will vary about the wisdom of this choice: some may see that this makes fighters more loyal to David because of his loyalty to all his fighters, while others may believe that this discourages men from doing their best in combat. David's practice may be neither completely wise nor completely foolish, but somewhere between the two.

Day 5 • 1 Samuel 31

21. Many of the soldiers of Israel run away, and Saul and his sons are overtaken and destroyed on Mount Gilboa.

22. Saul does not want to be captured by his enemies; he prefers the glory of dying on the battlefield than surviving as a loser and a prisoner.

23. The Bible presents no sign that God approves of such a choice. Saul's suicide is an act of despair, a result of his long-standing rebellion against God.

24. The Philistines, displaying actions common in ancient warfare, put the dead bodies on display and defile them as evidence of their victory. The men of Jabesh-gilead, a border town defended in the past by Saul, retrieve the bodies and burn them to prevent future defilement.

25. God protects David from harm even while His judgment is carried out against Saul and Saul's family. God brings upon Saul the punishment He has threatened. Throughout the Book of 1 Samuel, God's will is done as His people are defended and His enemies are overthrown. This does not always happen quickly, though, because God is patient even with sinners, giving them opportunities to repent.

The King Is Dead! Long Live the King!

2 Samuel 1–6

Preparing for the Session

Central Focus

Every king (or ruler), even a bad king, is a picture of Jesus, the King of kings.

Objectives

That participants, led by the Holy Spirit working through God's Word, will

1. recognize and imitate David's respect for those in authority;
2. exercise their own authority over others responsibly, remembering Jesus Christ, the source of all authority; and
3. honor Jesus as King of kings and Lord of lords.

For the Small-Group Leader

Small-Group Discussion Helps

Day 1 • 2 Samuel 1

1. The young man lied to make himself seem like the hero who killed King Saul and made it possible for David to claim the kingdom. He expected David to reward him for such an action.

2. Answers may vary. In this instance, David's responses are the opposite of what we would tend to expect. We would ordinarily expect him to be pleased that Saul had fallen and that the war was over. We would also expect him to reward the one who claimed to have killed Saul. But this is not how David reacts.

3. David shows his respect for Saul, and for the office of the king of Israel, by executing the man who claimed to have killed Saul. The Bible does not say whether David believed the young man's story, just that David was determined not to allow people to think that he was glad that Saul had died or that he intended to take advantage of Saul's death for his own ambitions.

4. First, David was sincerely sorry to learn about the death of his king, Saul, and of his friend, Jonathan. Second, David regretted the turmoil in Israel caused by the death of the king. Third, and least important, David wanted to avoid any appearance of seeking to take advantage of the death of the king to further his own ambitions.

5. We should be like God, not wishing anyone to suffer for their sins, but desiring to see all sinners repent and come to the knowledge of the truth. The judgment of God upon sinners should sadden us, even though we also rejoice to know that God triumphs over His enemies and protects His people from their persecutors.

Day 2 • 2 Samuel 2

6. David works hard to avoid any appearance of ambition and of taking what has not been voluntarily offered to him. One reason he is able to be patient and not assert his right to rule the kingdom is that he knows that God has promised the kingdom to him. Therefore, he is willing to wait for God's promise to be fulfilled precisely because he trusts the truth of that promise.

7. Abner probably does not know about God's promise to David or the anointing he received from Samuel. Abner might believe that the son of Saul has a better chance than David of uniting the twelve tribes under one king. Abner might also believe that the son of Saul will be easier to advise or to control than David would be.

8. They seek a limited conflict of twelve men from each side to decide the war, but all twenty-four men die, and war breaks out.

9. As a result of that failure, David's side prevails.

10. The personal feuds that result from the individual fighting do more to shape David's reign than the simple fact of his victory over the army of Israel.

Day 3 • 2 Samuel 3

11. Abner is insulted by Ish-bosheth and decides to change sides. He may have been contemplating that change and seeking an excuse to switch; the Bible does not describe all his motives and plans.

12. David welcomes Abner and treats him as an honored guest rather than an enemy. David clearly hopes

that he can unite the army and the nation through the decision of Abner to change sides. He also respects Abner's military ability and hopes to make use of it in the united army.

13. Joab murders Abner as a result of their family feud from the earlier fighting (in ch. 2). David responds to the murder by mourning publicly over the death of Abner and giving him a hero's burial.

14. By his public mourning, David shows that he was not guilty of plotting against Abner to seize the kingdom. He also wins the loyalty of those soldiers who respected and followed Abner. This final tribute to a fallen enemy, combined with his earlier respect for Saul, makes David the king of choice for most Israelites.

15. We should still reject sin and evil, even when they seem to benefit us. If we oppose only the sins that hurt us and not the sins that seem to benefit us, we reveal ourselves to be selfish rather than godly. When we oppose all sins equally, whether or not they help or harm us, we show ourselves to be on the side of God and of what is good rather than merely living for ourselves.

Day 4 • 2 Samuel 4–5

16. The captains hope to gain David's favor and rewards for their assassination of their king. They think that they can serve under David with special rewards for making it possible for him to rule all twelve tribes. They clearly have not been paying attention to David's reaction to the deaths of Saul, Jonathan, and Abner.

17. David executes the murderers for their assassination, just as he executed the man who claimed to have killed King Saul. Although David did not punish Joab for his murder of Abner, he did call down God's curses on Joab and his family.

18. They remember David's leadership in Israel's army before Saul became his enemy. They also remember God's promise to David.

19. David chooses a city that is near the middle of Israel and is outside of the land given to the tribe of Judah, his own tribe. Yet he also chooses a city that is familiar to him, since he grew up only a few miles away from Jerusalem. Finally, this city is still under the power of a Canaanite tribe, so David is able to make it his capital without taking it away from any of the tribes of Israel. He succeeds because of the overconfidence of the Jebusites and because he is familiar with the area; also, David succeeds because God is blessing him in all that he does.

20. David fights and conquers the Philistines and makes treaties with the Phoenicians. He builds a palace in Jerusalem that becomes a royal residence and a center of government. His wealth and his family increase while he lives in Jerusalem.

Day 5 • 2 Samuel 6

21. After making Jerusalem the center of government for the tribes of Israel, David wants to make the same city the center of religious observance. He also wants to ensure God's blessing upon himself and upon his rule.

22. David has the ark transported by cart rather than in the way God had commanded, carried by Levites using poles. God strikes dead the person who touches the ark without permission (even though that person meant only to do good) as a reminder that His people should follow His rules rather than making up their own rules in the service of God. God also emphasizes His holiness by defending the holiness of the ark, which represents His presence. David was both angry and afraid, but he learned his lesson and did not repeat this mistake.

23. David changes his mind when he sees that, when it is properly treated, the ark brings blessings instead of curses. This time, David has the ark carried in the way God had commanded, borne by Levites upon poles. He does this because God commanded it and because David had learned the hard way not to change what God had commanded. We learn also to respect holy things and to treat them with respect and according to God's commands rather than our own inclinations.

24. Michal, as the daughter of one king and wife of another, is unhappy to see the king do anything to lower the respect others might have for him, even if it is done to glorify God.

25. Because Michal speaks of her scorn, she has no children (no royal heirs to rule the kingdom after David is gone). The Bible does not say if this is the result of the Lord's judgment or a decision made by David.

You Are the Man!

2 Samuel 7–12

Preparing for the Session

Central Focus

As David sinned, repented, and was absolved, so also sinners today fall short of God's plan and cannot save themselves by what they do, but are redeemed by Christ.

Objectives

That participants, led by the Holy Spirit working through God's Word, will

1. identify the high cost of sin;
2. identify Jesus as the Redeemer who pays for the sins of the world; and
3. confess their sins and be confident of God's forgiveness through Christ.

For the Small-Group Leader

Small-Group Discussion Helps

Day 1 • 2 Samuel 7

1. David wants to build a temple in Jerusalem, a house for the Lord. He wants to do this because he feels it is wrong for him to live in a fine palace while the Lord's home is still a tent (which by now is more than four hundred years old).

2. The tabernacle was built according to God's commands, but God had never asked for a temple. God did not give David permission to build Him a house, since God had never asked for such a house.

3. God said that instead of letting David build Him a house, He would build a house for David. He would have safety from his enemies, a good reputation, and a peaceful kingdom. His son would then rule an eternal kingdom, being called by God a son.

4. Although in some small ways, Solomon appears to be the fulfillment of this promise, Solomon did not rule an eternal kingdom; Israel divided into two countries after Solomon died. Only Jesus is truly the Son of God; only Jesus rules an eternal kingdom.

5. David's prayer reflects his humility and the greatness of God. He knows that God's promises are true, and he also knows that they are spoken and fulfilled by grace and not because God's people deserve to receive His goodness.

Day 2 • 2 Samuel 8–9

6. David defeated and ruled the Philistines, the Moabites, the land of Zobah in the Euphrates River valley, the Syrians (or Arameans), the Edomites, and the Amalekites.

7. David now rules all the land promised to Abraham and his descendants.

8. This is not the final fulfillment of the promise given to Abraham, though, because a blessing must still come from his family living on this land that will bless all people. That blessing is Jesus, the Son of David and Son of God, who rules an eternal kingdom.

9. David shows his respect for the authority of Saul even after the death of Saul.

10. The respect that Christians show to rulers, even after those rulers are no longer in power, reflects the respect they have for God, the source of all authority. David also shows forgiveness for a former enemy in the way he treats Saul's grandson.

Day 3 • 2 Samuel 10

11. David intended to keep his agreement with the Ammonites when their king died and his son succeeded him on the throne.

12. David had sent ambassadors as a gesture of peaceful goodwill, but the Ammonite princes suspected David's ambassadors of being spies.

13. The Ammonites embarrassed and disgraced David's ambassadors, leading to war between Ammon and Israel. The Ammonites allied themselves with the Syrians (Arameans) to fight against David and the Israelites.

14. This alliance was perhaps Israel's largest war under David, but the Israelites defeated the combined power of Aram and Ammon. (Thus Ammon can be added to the list of defeated nations from 2 Samuel 8.)

15. The main reason for David's success was that God was blessing him and was keeping His promises to David and to Israel—promises that went all the way back to God's covenant with Abraham, Isaac, and Jacob.

Day 4 • 2 Samuel 11

16. David coveted his neighbor's wife (Tenth Commandment), committed adultery (Sixth Commandment), bore false witness against his neighbor (Eighth Commandment), and then murdered his neighbor (Fifth Commandment). In all these things, he showed that his desires mattered more to him than obedience to God (First Commandment).

17. David did not mean to see Bathsheba bathing on the rooftop, so he might have said that coveting his neighbor's wife was an accident. The adultery resulted from the coveting, from the fact that as king he had the power to fulfill his desires, but also from her willingness to commit the same sin. The false witness was an attempt to hide the adultery and its results. The murder was a consequence of the failure of the false witness to conceal the adultery, as well as a result of David's pride as king and his anger that his previous plans to escape the appearance of guilt had not been successful. And, ultimately, David was putting his own desires above those of the Lord.

18. Sinners often claim to be helpless in a chain of events, unable to break out of a sinful pattern. Only Christ's forgiveness can break the chains of sin and end sinful patterns.

19. Answers will vary. Many examples can be offered of sins adding to sins, especially later sins caused by the wish to avoid the blame of earlier sins.

20. Joab obeyed David's command to risk the life of Uriah, but he still knew that what he was doing by the king's command was wrong; he knew that David would have been right to express anger. David was not angry because he got what he wanted—the death of Uriah.

Day 5 • 2 Samuel 12

21. Nathan tells a story about a rich man who steals a poor man's sheep to prepare his challenge of David's sin. This preparation was necessary because of the power of the king to punish his enemies, and because David is more likely to use that power to protect himself from the just punishment of God than he would use it against a real enemy.

22. Nathan's goal was to lead David to repentance and to announce absolution. The real purpose of this conversation is in verse 13, where Nathan says to David, "The Lord also has put away your sin; you will not die."

23. Like Nathan, Christians must warn sinners of the consequence of their sins, not to judge and condemn them, but to lead them into repentance and to tell them that Jesus has paid for their sins on the cross. Like Nathan, Christians sometimes need to be creative in the ways that they present the Law to sinners, because the direct approach is not always effective. Christians find it difficult to talk about sin with sinners because they fear anger and rejection. We also know that we too are sinners, and we would rather not be reminded of our sins.

24. When David heard that the baby was going to die, he grieved and fasted and begged God for the child's life. When he heard that the baby had died, he ended his fast and returned to life as normal. He knew God's mercy and hoped that God would grant life to the baby, but after the baby had died, David knew that the fact of the child's death could not be changed. Other people found this behavior strange because normally people grieve after a death, rather than grieving before a death and not grieving afterward.

25. David's son died at the age of six days, before he had been circumcised. David was a man of faith who expected to wait in paradise with Jesus for the resurrection to eternal life. His confidence that his uncircumcised son would also be in paradise and at the resurrection comforts Christian parents of children who die in the womb or shortly after birth without being baptized; they can hope, like David, to see those children in paradise and at the resurrection to eternal life.

Absalom, O Absalom

2 Samuel 13–19

Preparing for the Session

Central Focus

A rebellious son who dies in battle becomes a picture of God's sinless Son who dies to pay for the world's rebellion.

Objectives

That participants, led by the Holy Spirit working through God's Word, will

1. recognize the sins of Absalom;

2. perceive how Absalom the son of David can, in spite of his sins, be a picture of Jesus Christ the Son of David; and

3. find their own sins and rebellion crucified with Christ and buried with Him.

For the Small-Group Leader

Small-Group Discussion Helps

Day 1 • 2 Samuel 13

1. God's Word contains ugly narratives like this chapter for three reasons: (a) They show the goodness of God and of His commands as compared to the ugliness of sin and its consequences. (b) They remind us of our sins and show us the ugly consequences of the wrong things we have done. (c) They highlight the glory of the Gospel, showing how great a power was needed to overturn sin and all its consequences. Reading about these events today, we learn not to minimize or romanticize sinful behavior, but rather to recognize it and to seek God's answer to the world's evil.

2. Amnon coveted a woman who could not be his wife. He lied to her, raped her, and then rejected her, increasing the disgrace of his previous sins. Amnon committed these sins because he was tempted to fulfill his own desires. Pride also made him believe that he could have whatever he wanted and do whatever he wanted. His friend and cousin Jonadab encouraged Amnon in these sins.

3. David was very angry, but he said nothing about the sin. Unlike Nathan, who was bold enough to confront David and call for repentance, David was afraid to speak about sin within his own family, especially the sin of the heir to the throne. David had been strong enough not to seek revenge against Saul when Saul sinned against David, but that strength becomes weakness when he, as king, should rebuke the sins of his own son.

4. Absalom deceives and murders his brother Amnon. He commits these sins seeking revenge for Amnon's sins against Tamar. The revenge of Absalom is sinful, nonetheless.

5. David allows Absalom to flee. Once again, he does nothing, even though it is his job as king to punish sinners. David's weakness in responding to sin may be a result of his awareness of his own guilt, but David abandons his responsibilities as king by not responding to these sins.

Day 2 • 2 Samuel 14–15

6. Joab seeks to have David recall Absalom from exile. He may be imitating the prophet Nathan's call for repentance when David had sinned with Bathsheba. Joab is looking toward the future of Israel; he wants the strongest figure available to rule the kingdom when David dies, and clearly he views Absalom as a strong ruler—perhaps because Absalom sought revenge against Amnon while David remained silent.

7. Absalom sets Joab's fields on fire to get his attention and beg him to reconcile him to his father. This destruction of property was sinful, even though it did accomplish Absalom's purpose. It reveals once again his pride and his belief that anything he does is acceptable because he is the son and heir of the king.

8. Absalom breaks both the Fourth (Honor your father and your mother) and Eighth (You shall not give false testimony against your neighbor) Commandments by suggesting that he would be a better king and judge than his father, David.

9. David apparently believes that he and his faithful soldiers are not strong enough to win a civil war against Absalom. As events later in the book will show, David is also not willing to harm Absalom, even though Absa-

lom is rebelling against his father and against the proper government of Israel.

10. Many soldiers and officers remain faithful to David, including Ittai from Gath (a Philistine city), Abiathar and Zadok the priests, and Hushai the Archite. David allows Ittai and his soldiers to accompany him. He has the priests remain in Jerusalem; he also has Hushai remain to give bad advice to Absalom and so improve David's chances of recapturing the city and the nation.

Day 3 • 2 Samuel 16

11. Both Mephibosheth and Shimei seem to show disloyalty toward David.

12. Mephibosheth seems disloyal by failing to accompany David; his servant Ziba reports that Mephibosheth hopes to be crowned king in David's place. Shimei seems disloyal to David by cursing him and throwing stones at him as he leaves Jerusalem.

13. David believes that he deserves to be cursed; he believes that Shimei may be obeying a command from God to speak these curses, and David does not want to do anything that would be unfaithful to God.

14. Hushai suggests that Absalom demonstrate his takeover of David's power by sleeping openly with David's ten concubines that were left behind at the palace.

15. Nathan the prophet had told David this would happen as part of the consequence of his sin with Bathsheba (2 Samuel 12:11).

Day 4 • 2 Samuel 17

16. Ahithophel advises a quick attack. Hushai (who is secretly helping David) advises that Absalom wait until he can gather all his forces. Absalom believes that Hushai's advice is better and does not try for a quick attack.

17. Although Absalom has time to strengthen himself, David also has time to gather his forces and prepare to be attacked. In the end, this time of preparation will give David the victory over Absalom.

18. Ahithophel commits suicide. Perhaps he is concerned that he has lost his job with both kings—with David by serving Absalom, and with Absalom by having his advice rejected in favor of Hushai's advice. Perhaps he perceives that, because of the delay, David will win and he will be punished for working with Absalom.

19. God's name is mentioned only as a possible source of Shimei's decision to curse David. Most of the people in these chapters are doing what seems right to them without consulting the Lord or seeking His will.

20. God keeps His promise to protect David from his enemies in spite of the fact that David does not seem to be consulting God or relying on His promise.

Day 5 • 2 Samuel 18–19

21. David asks his soldiers not to hurt his son Absalom. This weakens them, as they will not be able to conduct an all-out war while obeying this command. It probably also reduces their morale, since they are fighting for David against a rebel, and David himself seems to favor the rebel.

22. Absalom's hair becomes entangled in a tree, and Joab and his soldiers strike him dead. Moses had pronounced a curse on anyone who dies hanging from a tree (Deuteronomy 21:23). Absalom dies because of his pride, which caused him to rebel against David, but which also caused him to have such hair on his head that he could be entangled in the branches of a tree.

23. Joab is able to divide the good news of victory from the bad news (from David's perspective) of the death of Absalom. David is not very happy about his victory because he wants to hear that Absalom survived; he grieves and mourns when he learns that Absalom is dead.

24. Joab advises David to welcome his troops and celebrate the victory with them, in spite of his sadness over the death of Absalom. If David fails to reward his faithful fighters, they will not remain faithful. David does as Joab suggests, but he then fires Joab as commander of the forces.

25. David pardons Shimei for his curses. This forgiveness is wise, as it reminds everyone of God's forgiveness for sinners. He divides the estate of Mephibosheth between Mephibosheth and Ziba, even though he had previously given the entire estate to Ziba when Ziba claimed that Mephibosheth was hoping to take the throne. This may also be considered wise, because it prevented a long investigation to see which of the men had lied, but it punishes the honest man by taking away half his wealth while rewarding the liar by granting him half the estate.

Number the People

2 Samuel 20–24

Preparing for the Session

Central Focus

By grace, God converts the sinful census of Israel and its consequences into an opportunity for His love and mercy to prevail at the site of the temple.

Objectives

That participants, led by the Holy Spirit working through God's Word, will

1. perceive the subtle distinction between temptation and testing;
2. recognize the sin of pride in David's arbitrary census; and
3. see how grace triumphs over judgment in David's life and in their lives.

For the Small-Group Leader

Small-Group Discussion Helps

Day 1 • 2 Samuel 20

1. The leader of the rebellion is described as "a worthless man" (v. 1), but clearly he is able to capitalize on the discontent sown by Absalom, which was increased by David's halfhearted acceptance of his army's victory.

2. Joab assassinated the man who had replaced him as commander of David's forces so he could return to the position of commander.

3. This death and change of command slowed David's forces, but in the end they still prevailed.

4. When David's forces were ready to sack the city, a "wise woman" persuaded the city leaders to surrender Sheba and end the sack.

5. Answers will vary, but may include some of the following: Possibly Sheba was worthless, since his rebellion showed him to be disloyal to the king. Also, we can note that his disloyalty to King David suggests a disloyalty to God. We can also note that elsewhere in the Old Testament (e.g., Deuteronomy 13:13), "worthless" is used to describe Israelites who have abandoned God to follow the false gods of the Caananites.

Day 2 • 2 Samuel 21

6. Saul's guilt was hanging over Israel because he had wrongly put some Gibeonites to death. Because the leader of the nation has sinned, the entire nation is under judgment. Guilt can be transferred from one to many.

7. Since Saul has already died, some of his descendants are to be put to death to atone for his sin. Guilt can be transferred from one to several. The price of guilt can be removed by the suffering of those to whom it is transferred.

8. The death of Jesus on the cross is pictured. The guilt of many is transferred to one, and the price of guilt is paid by the one to whom it is transferred.

9. God is said to visit "the iniquity of the fathers on the children to the third and fourth generation" (Exodus 20:5). Participants may think of many examples of guilt lingering and tainting others.

10. The principle of sacrifice is that one being can pay for the sins of another. If that were not possible, then everyone who sins would be punished for that sin. While that seems more just than the principle of sacrifice, it means that no one could be saved from guilt, and forgiveness could not exist. The principles of shared guilt and sacrifice make possible the redemption of the cross, which rescues sinners from their guilt and grants them eternal life.

Day 3 • 2 Samuel 22

11. Music can make a message more memorable. It communicates to a different part of the human mind than words alone.

12. Answers might include the anger of the Lord in verses 8–16, the mention of rules and statutes in verse 23, and God's response to people that varies according to their nature in verses 26–27.

13. It should be noted that David's claim to be righteous and blameless in verses 21–25 is a result of the grace of God. David had sinned, but God had removed his sins.

14. Answers might include the names of God in verses 2–3, His answer to David's prayer in verse 7, His rescue of David in verses 17–20, and the final promise of verses 50–51.

15. David's song makes it clear to us that we can be certain of our salvation. Answers will vary, but may include the following: The Lord is shown here to be almighty; no one, not even the worst of our enemies, can disrupt His plans for us. God deals with His people according to righteousness, rather than judgment.

Day 4 • 2 Samuel 23

16. David remembers the promise of his house, the promise that a Son of David will rule an eternal kingdom.

17. Some died and were replaced by others. There were never more than thirty in this special team, but, over the course of forty years, more than thirty men served.

18. Great victories against the Philistines and against Moab; the killing of many enemies; and a special raid in which water was brought from the well of Bethlehem because David spoke of his desire to drink that water. He refused to drink it, though, because it had been brought to him through an unnecessary risk.

19. The last name is Uriah, the husband of Bathsheba, whose death was the deliberate result of one of David's commands.

20. The reader is reminded of David's sin and also of God's forgiveness.

Day 5 • 2 Samuel 24

21. The usual answer is that David is showing his pride by wanting to count the number of people that he rules. Another suggestion is that David should have collected an offering to the Lord along with this census (as Moses did in the Book of Numbers) and that his failure to gather money for the Lord was the sinful aspect of the census.

22. David and Israel can face three years of famine, three months of fleeing the attack of an enemy, or three days of pestilence.

23. David has faced the first two situations in the past. He chooses the pestilence as "the hand of the Lord" rather than the danger that comes from enemies. David knows that the Lord will be merciful; he has no such confidence that human enemies would be merciful.

24. David repents, and God relents and cuts short the judgment. This indicates that David did choose wisely (although either of the other two judgments could have been cut short by the power of the Lord as well).

25. David buys land and builds an altar at the place where Solomon, David's son, will build the temple. An event of mercy and grace becomes the impetus for a place of mercy and grace for many generations of God's people.